(Somatic) for Kari Edwards (1954-2006)

meditation with 7 of the 14 different incense sticks she gave me

OPIUM — DAY 6 ↑ BINAH

LEMONGRASS — DAY 5 ↑ DISPEL

VIOLET, AFRICAN, JASMINE

CEDAR — DAY ONE ↗ MERCURY

MYRRH, GARDE — DAY 7 ISIS

MUSK, SANDALWOOD — DAY 3 ↑ SATURN

FRANKINCENSE — DAY TWO ↑ exhaled homage

EUCALYPTUS — DAY 4 HEALTH

YLANG-YLANG, ROSE, PATCHOULI,

Find the CD that Christina Strong made as the one Kari gave me has a skip. Skips on 3rd track. NO SKIPS! Kari's music, the incense. How long before sadness cuts through to joy? One day at a time. Eat only brown rice, seaweed, miso and rancha before meditating. Use the large white candle, the 8-day white candle. Write Kari's name along the shaft. Do these BEFORE house sitting in 2 weeks, but 7 consecutive days!

Toes Will Know!

this is about being free by seeing how we are not free. The liver, the heart, kidneys, sciatic nerve in foot reflexology. Sex glands back by the heel.

CLENCHING toes for each moment of dishonesty: white lies, smiling when you don't want to, being polite to RUD customers at work!

lungs — brain stem
neck muscles
liver
(anger stored) — kidneys
sex glands

CLENCHING will activate all the pressu points at once! Allow the points to take the brunt of these actions. Take note for the clenching, take more notes while soaking feet at night. Allow the salt water to absorb these man moments of the day — A RELEASE

7 days? Last day STUDY feet with a magnifying glass.

PENNY & JUICE

Wash a penny and put it under your
tongue then set out to the streets.
Copper is Aphrodite's metal. ~~its ore is~~
Drink oranges, these are her fruit,
the goddess of love binds on citrus.

Find a place to sit and meditate.
What is the best love of your life
thus far?

Put the penny on your head, as copper
(or heart chakra) has been activating
the tongue. Now on the crown
chakra it will illuminate further for
the note-taking

crown
tongue

heart
chakra

Then write about poverty and
deprivation for the love known.

making four times the amount of
noise forecast from the outset
HELLO is not enough to set in
to break open

ELVIS and the MRI

thinking of Hannah Weiner seeing words on foreheads and having spirit guides.

The MRI has an enormous magnetic instrument which PULLS protons of our body water in one direction for a clear image to be taken of body tissue. The thumping can follow a meditation on music by Elvis as Elvis music is used all over the world to heal bodies and broken spirits. The chamber can be entered as one enters a ritualistic cave.

Prep with crystal-infused water and studying a room to visit when inside the MRI

and inside that NOISE it makes.
The noise can gather the mind
into the point of physical
departure for visiting THE
studied room.

CRYSTAL MAPPING

Draw map of blocks surrounding the apartment for the crystal toss.

⊛ stone toss — CHESTNUT ST.

⊛ home — SANSOM ST.

WALNUT St.

23rd St.   22nd St.   21st St.

AMETHYST: psychic protection — calming — nervous system — bolsters memory functions

Meditate on stone's properties. Then toss it onto the map.

Go to location with the stone and incorporate stone properties with surrounding landscape.

A Nude in the doorway

When alone at home stand in a bucket of room-temperature water naked. Keep a pen and notepad nearby. Get comfortable standing in water naked at the door. Look through the peep hole for a long time to study the world outside the door. I asked Rich to come over and knock and say "Are you naked in your bucket of water?"

STRETCH, be quiet. Sit on floor and write, then pause to make 4 SHARP whistles. Clears the air. Write again. Pause, whistle. Write, pause, whistle. STRETCH, repeat.

What were the details of the doorway never before noticed?.

What outside?. How NEW will this now be, this place?. Reinvented home space.

A BEAUTIFUL

MARSUPIAL

AFTERNOON

CACONRAD

WAVE BOOKS SEATTLE & NEW YORK

A BEAUTIFUL MARSUPIAL AFTERNOON

NEW (SOMA)TICS

PUBLISHED BY WAVE BOOKS

WWW.WAVEPOETRY.COM

WAVE BOOKS TITLES ARE DISTRIBUTED TO THE TRADE BY

CONSORTIUM BOOK SALES AND DISTRIBUTION

PHONE: 800-283-3572 / SAN 631-760X

THIS TITLE IS AVAILABLE IN A LIMITED EDITION

DIRECTLY FROM THE PUBLISHER.

LIBRARY OF CONGRESS CATALOGING-IN-PUBLICATION DATA

CONRAD, C. A.

A BEAUTIFUL MARSUPIAL AFTERNOON / C.A. CONRAD. — 1ST ED.

P. CM.

ISBN 978-1-933517-59-9 (ALK. PAPER)

I. TITLE.

PS3603.O555B43 2012

811'.6—DC23

2011035008

DESIGNED AND COMPOSED BY QUEMADURA

PRINTED IN THE UNITED STATES OF AMERICA

9 8 7 6 5 4

THE LIVING AND THE DEAD GIVE IN AND WAVE TO ME

—DESNOS

THIS BOOK IS FOR MY FRIENDS

WHO TEACH ME MUCH AND

FOR MY ENEMIES WHO

TEACH ME THE REST

A BEAUTIFUL

MARSUPIAL

AFTERNOON

THE RIGHT TO
MANIFEST MANIFESTO

INTRODUCTION TO (SOMA)TIC POETRY EXERCISES
AND THE RESULTING POEMS

I cannot stress enough how much this mechanistic world, as it becomes more and more efficient, resulting in ever increasing brutality, has required me to FIND MY BODY to FIND MY PLANET in order to find my poetry. If I am an extension of this world then I am an extension of garbage, shit, pesticides, bombed and smoldering cities, microchips, cyber, astral and biological pollution, BUT ALSO the beauty of a patch of unspoiled sand, all that croaks from the mud, talons on the cliff that take rock and silt so seriously flying over the spectacle for a closer examination are nothing short of necessary. The most idle-looking pebble will suddenly match any hunger, any rage. Suddenly, and will be realized at no other speed than suddenly.

(Soma)tic poetry is a praxis I've developed to more fully engage the everyday through writing. *Soma* is an Indo-Persian word that means "the divine." *Somatic* is Greek. Its meaning translates as "the tissue" or "nervous system." The goal is to coalesce soma and somatic, while triangulating patterns of experience with the world around us. Experiences that are unorthodox steps in the writing process can shift the poet's perception of the quotidian, if only for a series of moments. This offers an opportunity to see the details clearer. Through music, dirt, food, scent, taste, in storms, in bed, on the subway and at the grocery store, (Soma)tic Exercises and the poems that result are just waiting to be utilized or invented, everywhere, and anytime.

The last large wild beasts are being hunted, poisoned, asphyxiated in one way or another, and the transmission of their wildness is dying, taming. A desert is rising with this falling pulse. It is our duty as poets and others who have not lost our jagged, creative edges to FILL that gap, and RESIST the urge to subdue our spirits and lose ourselves in the hypnotic beep of machines, of war, in the banal need for power, and things. With our poems and creative core, we must RETURN THIS WORLD to its seismic levels of wildness.

The aim of (Soma)tic poetry and poetics is the realization of two basic ideas: (1) Everything around us has a creative viability with the potential to spur new modes of thought and imaginative output. (2) The most vital ingredient to bringing sustainable, humane changes to our world is creativity. This can be enacted on a daily basis.

It's ALL Collaboration. Anyone who ever fed you, loved you, anyone who ever made you feel unworthy, stupid, ugly, anyone who made you express doubt or assuredness, every one of these helped make you. Those who learn to speak with authority to mask their own self-loathing, those may be the deepest influences on us. But they are part of us. And we have each fit together uniquely as a result, and so there are no misshapen forms as all are misshapen forms, from tyrants to wallflowers. Every poem written is filtered through the circumstances of the poet, through the diet of the poet. Just as unique is every reader of poems, for a thousand different readers of a poem equals a thousand different poems. We are here relying on one another whether or not we wish it. There are no poets writing in quiet caves because every poet is a human being as misshapen as any other human being. The room can be as quiet as possible, earplugs can be administered, but the poet still has a parade of influence running inside from one ear to the other. The quiet room cannot blot them out; it can however help the poet listen closer to this music for their own creation. We are not alone in our particular stew of molecules and the sooner we admit, even admire the influence of this world, the freer we will be to construct new chords of thought without fear.

ANOINT THYSELF

—FOR JOHN COLETTI & JESS MYNES

Visit the home of a deceased poet you admire and bring some natural thing back with you. I went to Emily Dickinson's house the day after a reading event with my friend Susie Timmons. I scraped dirt from the foot of huge trees in the backyard into a little pot. We then drove into the woods where we found miniature pears, apples, and cherries to eat. I meditated in the arms of an oak tree with the pot of Emily's dirt, waking to the flutter of a red cardinal on a branch a foot or so from my face, staring, showing me his little tongue.

When I returned to Philadelphia I didn't shower for three days, then rubbed Emily's dirt all over my body, kneaded her rich Massachusetts soil deeply into my flesh, then put on my clothes and went out into the world. Every once in a while I stuck my nose inside the neck of my shirt to inhale her delicious, sweet earth covering me. I felt revirginized through the ceremony of my senses, I could feel her power tell me these are the ways to walk and speak and shift each glance into total concentration for maximum usage of our little allotment of time on a planet. LOSE AND WASTE NO MORE TIME POET! Lose and waste no more time she said to me as I took note after note on the world around me for the poem.

EMILY DICKINSON
CAME TO EARTH and
THEN SHE LEFT

your sweaty party dress and my sweaty party
dress lasted a few minutes until the tomato
was gone someday they will disambiguate
you but not while I'm around our species
won Emily we won it feels so good to be win-
ning the flame of victory pass it around it
never goes out dinosaurs ruled Massachu-
setts dinosaurs fucking and laying eggs in
Amherst Boston Mount Holyoke then you
appeared high priestess pulling it out of the
goddamned garden with both hands you
Emily remembered the first time compre-
hending a struck match can spread a flame it
feels good to win this fair and square protest
my assessment all you want but not needing
to dream is like not needing to see the world
awaken to itself indestructible epiphanies
consume the path and just because you're
having fun doesn't mean you're not going to
die recrimination is the fruit to defy with un-
expected appetite I will be your outsider if
that's how you need me electric company's
stupid threatening letters cannot affect a poet
who has faced death

4

Séance Your Own Way

This particular exercise is meant to encourage anyone wishing to communicate with loved ones who have met their deaths. A month before my friend kari edwards died she gave me a packet of incense made in the community of India where she and her life-partner, Fran Blau, had lived for a short time. It was a sampler packet with 14 different scents. After kari died the incense produced a force field of psychic barbed wire on my desk. She had given me this gift just before hugging me goodbye and getting on an airplane that would fly her away from Philadelphia for the last time. After news of her death, burning the incense, even TOUCH-ING the incense would seem an extraordinary event. Then I decided that there was NO BETTER WAY to communicate with a dead poet you loved than through the process of creating poetry with them, and for them.

I chose 7 of the 14 different incense sticks, using the number 7 because as a symbol it is de-signed for energy to rise up the stem and fly off the top, the top serving as a very determined, preternatural catapult. This is why 7 is a number of good fortune, as it sends messages, wishes, whatever's put into it STRAIGHT into the air. For 7 days I would meditate with each of the 7 scents, and I chose the order of the scents for a transmission magic spell, a kind of supernatural broadcast. For instance, DAY 1: CEDAR is a scent of the god Mercury, used to close the gap of time and space between you and the one you wish to contact. DAY 2: FRANKINCENSE is a tree resin used to purify and honor the divine. DAY 3: MUSK, a scent associated with the planet Saturn to aid in making inquiries into evolution-ary spiritual responsibilities on Earth. DAY 4: EUCALYPTUS is used for many things, but in this case I was using it to firm my own resolve to become macrobiotic again, telling kari that I wanted to and needed to return to total health (it worked, as I've been macrobiotic for 6 months now). DAY 5: LEMONGRASS is used to dispel negative charges left behind after the healing resolutions of eucalyptus. DAY 6: OPIUM invokes Binah on the Tree of Life, and Binah helps the questioner understand information, and in this case understand more clearly what the messages from kari for the poems mean. DAY 7: MYRRH is the scent of the goddess Isis, The High Priestess, and I could think of no better way to honor kari than with the scent of Isis, She the great patron of nature and art, and She who puts the dead back together. Each day I would UNPLUG THE PHONE, create a quiet space, then put kari's music CD (experimental electronic music she created) on, then burn the incense, and WAIT IN THAT SPACE for the words to come.

kari7

(SEVEN MEDITATIONS WITH INCENSE FROM
KARI EDWARDS BROUGHT BACK FROM SRI
AUROBINDO ASHRAM, PONDICHERRY, INDIA)

*after I am reborn, I'll try to read or write in a quiet place where the
pigs can't get in and the cats send letters, it's really just too much . . .
I truly can't face the world until I have slowly entered. I don't know if
it's just me or not, but I can't come from ten thousand leagues under
the sea to the present . . .* —kari edwards, from *a diary of lies*

CEDAR

pencil
making arrows
to the pain

green
washed from
liver
by the fire

7

FRANKINCENSE

it is a tired
position on
the map
can you afford the wait?

be asked first they
told us but
someone must
tell them to
ask *so fuck it!*

MUSK

dormancy entered a flayed
bond by
soda fountains of the world it
seems funny but it is
exactly funny how
exceptions cram
into the disappear

EUCALYPTUS

a streetlight shows
its pole for miles

(*send message to kari*)
you missed the man
flying across the
English Channel by
backpack jet in 2008
it was on the news

LEMONGRASS

you laughed when
I suggested introducing
spitting cobras
to the parks
of Philadelphia

you introduced a chip
from corn grown
in Iowa

OPIUM

spider lowers
on silk from
your finger

you vouch for
the fly about
to escape

MYRRH

I'm a poet not a
motivational speaker

someone told me I can't
hate death without
hating life *they're so full of shit!*
I'm hating death
looking for you between the
microscope and telescope

WAKE UP AND UPDATE YOUR BLOG DAMMIT!

WHITE HELIUM

— FOR SHARON MESMER

Take a white helium balloon with a red string into a private room where no one can see you or bother you. Don't even let them know you have it, and hide it in a closet when it's not in use. You need 4 consecutive days for this exercise. DAY 1: chew your favorite gum while naked in bed, or on the floor, but on your back, arms behind your head, legs spread apart, relaxed, with your balloon on the ceiling above you. After your gum is sufficiently chewed and soft, stick the end of the red string into the gum, then shove the gum into your navel. WORK IT IN THERE. Relax again with the balloon above you, now attached to your navel. Navels are scars from birth, scars that are the center of gravity. Take notes about your navel now filled with gum and balloon string. MOTHER FED YOU through this before you were born, chocolates, spaghetti, tangerines, mayonnaise and turnips and cashews and pickled beets! You processed shit and other excretions through this, YOU LIVED THROUGH THIS HOLE WITH THE BALLOON NOW HOLDING ON! Take many notes.

DAY 2: sit naked on the floor while holding the balloon to your forehead, rub it into your third eye, bouncing your head gently into it over and over. Hum into it while thinking about your day, especially something that might have irritated you; hum LOUDER when irritating thoughts come to mind. Take notes. Now tie the red string around your penis, if you don't have a penis tie it around a dildo inserted into your vagina, or around your thigh, then walk around with your balloon bouncing above you. Read a favorite VERY FAVORITE book of poetry, stopping from time to time to take notes about reading this book naked with your balloon attached to you. How is it different reading this book naked with your balloon? Now read your favorite poem in the book backwards out loud, last word first, even read the title backwards. Take notes.

DAY 3: cut a little hair from your head and pubic hair, and tape it to your balloon. Let the balloon rest on the ceiling while you sit on the floor naked, looking up at your bits of hair above you. Bring your balloon down slowly and study the hair and let it float back to the ceiling. Bring it down again and WITHOUT THINKING ABOUT WHAT TO DRAW draw spontaneous drawings with several differently colored magic markers. Let it float back to the ceiling. While it's on the ceiling take notes about what you've just drawn. What does it look like? How do you feel about what you've drawn? Take notes about each color and how you used each color. Bring your balloon back down by the string and study it closer.

DAY 4: smear snot or blood or semen or pussy juice or earwax or piss or vomit or shit or spit or sweat or whatever excretion you have available onto your balloon. Hold on to the string as it floats above you. Relax on your back on the floor. Hold the string by your toes with your legs extended. Look at the balloon with binoculars. What emblem is this? What Jolly Roger? What letter of love or apology is this? What declaration? Take notes, take notes. Slowly let the air out and put the balloon with all the hair and drawings and secretions into a sock, and put the sock under your pillow. In the morning take notes about dreams you had, especially if the balloon appeared. Your excretions had just been floating above you the night before, what was in your dreams?

every weakness of the world in
ONE LIMB FOR A DAY

fighting impulse to interpret another
suicide's intentions

a jab at the oldest place we
could find in the sometime of
temporal sometime

the band played "You've
Lost That Lovin' Feelin'" at
the wedding

his ass the
template of
my life

glaciers melting as my
interest in ice hockey grows

I cannot recalibrate the
runaway graph of
these opposites

Poland came back
after disappearing
(geography's much
easier through war)

                              waiting for the
                               bus I let it
                              go to keep in
                               the poem

              these residual hauntings
              sound redundant
                        until they visit
                     no more

                            maps born
              headfirst from war

                 I am talking about
                  real equality
                   the equality of economics

hideous words in computer
                          code
                                  avalanche compassionate
                                                    stasis

              the compulsion to reproduce
              I don't have it
              you weren't born
              you can't hear me say I'm glad

                         maps bathed in
                          testosterone in utero

an unexpected pint of blood
shot from the engine

I will die angry for dying
I will resist
I am going to
resist I am
resistance in the making
visit cancer wards take notes for the war ahead

I want to be here to
meet YOU new
beautiful friend

wondering how to love
this world without
sounding silly?
ah, too late

DIGIT COGNIZANCE

Take account of how many times you're not saying or doing EXACTLY what you want to say or do in a day. How many times do you use a tone in your voice that is not honest? How many times are you polite when you want TO SCREAM? How much compromise does your day comprise? Take CLOSE account of this. DON'T LIE ABOUT IT EITHER! This is for you, no one else will know SO BE TOTALLY HONEST! What is your body like when you're not being who you are? How does it feel? Are your hands doing something in particular each time? Your feet? Your groin, your stomach—how does your body react when you are not REALLY you? At the end of the day take notes about this. These notes will be the formal outline for this exercise.

FOR THE NEXT 7 days you will pay attention to the SIGNS OF DISHONESTY in your voice and your body, and whenever you are not who you REALLY WANT TO BE at any moment in the day. Each time you are being polite to your boss, or the babysitter, or don't say FUCK because there's a child in the room, EACH TIME you are not you, CLENCH YOUR TOES! CLENCH THEM! Every time, CLENCH THEM! At the end of the day are your toes tired of this? Are they feeling BETTER maybe? Soak your feet in hot salt water and WRITE WRITE WRITE as quickly as you can, EACH NIGHT for 7 nights after a day of TOE-CLENCHING DISHONESTY soak them in hot salt water and WRITE at the pace only a FURIOUS YOU would know how to do! OPEN YOUR EYES wider than they're used to being open and WRITE, WRITE WITHOUT BLINKING if you can. WRITE! At the end of 7 days take a long time staring at your feet, your toes, look at them. Stick them in your face if you can, right up to your face and look at them. Take a magnifying glass and look at your feet. For 7 days your toes have been taking the brunt of your dishonest actions. How does that look? Take notes. How does that feel? Take many notes. STICK YOUR TOES IN YOUR MOUTH if you can. How does that taste?

MILD ENEMY LOTION

do not sleep bundle unfurled
      sleep
         less sleep less paint fire on car drive long as miles last
                  tension envelops us no more
we stopped taking more than needed was the
Science of Love sleep less sew flags for imagi-
nary nations much more human in our listening
RADAR ATTENTIVE DRIVING
INTO AMERICA fresh fire painted at state
line smell pictures of flowers *eyes can smell them*
sleep less we are lessons bird knows coming up
into air bird knows every ray we examine is more
vintage than the next these impressions of hope
give us total immersion sleep less everyone is two
places here and in memory hold porches to their
light vantage ourselves at garment awareness
sleep less hold breath open let us keep our hours

Storm SOAKED Bread

—FOR JULIAN BROLASKI

Sit outside under shelter of a doorway, pavilion, or umbrella on a park bench, but somewhere outside where you can easily touch, smell, taste, FEEL the storm. Lean your face into the weather, face pointed UP to the sky, stay there for a bit with eyes closed while water fills the wells of your eyes. Come back into the shelter properly baptized in the beauty of pure elements and be quiet and still for a few minutes. Take some preliminary notes about your surroundings. Try not to engage with others who might run to your shelter for cover. If they insist on talking MOVE somewhere else; you are a poet with a storm to digest, this isn't time for small talk! You are not running from the storm, you are opening to it, you are IN IT! Stick a bare arm or foot into the storm, let your skin take in a meditative measure of wind and rain. If you are someone who RAN from storms in the past take time to examine the joys of the experience. Remind yourself you are a human being who is approximately 80 percent water SO WHAT'S THE HARM OF A FEW DROPS ON THE OUTSIDE!? Right? YES! Pause, hold your breath for a count of 4, then write with a FURY and without thinking, just let it FLOW OUT OF YOU, write, write, WRITE!

Set an empty cup in the storm, hold a slice of bread in the storm. Then put a little salt and pepper on your storm soaked bread, maybe some oregano and garlic. With deliberate SLOOOWNESS chew your storm bread and drink the storm captured in your cup. Slowly. So, slowly, please, with, a, slowness, that, is, foreign, to, you. THINK the whole slow time of chewing and drinking how this water has been in a cycle for MILLIONS OF YEARS, falling to earth, quenching horses, elephants, lizards, dinosaurs, humans. They pissed, they died, their water evaporated and gathered again into clouds to drizzle down AND STORM DOWN into rivers, puddles, aqueducts, and ancient cupped hands.

Humans who LOVED, who are long dead, humans who thieved, raped, murdered, were generous, playful, disappointed, fearful, annoyed and adored one another, each of them dying in their own way, their water going back to the sky, coming back down to your bread, your lips, your stomach, to feed your sinew, your brain, your living, beautiful day. Take your notes POET, IT IS YOUR MOMENT to be totally aware, completely awake!

ONE DAY I WILL STEP FROM THE BEAUTY PARLOR AND ENLIST IN THE FREQUENCY OF STARLINGS

my favorite morning
is not caring if
blood on sheets
is yours or mine

a machine in
your station
rides me
tracks to snacks
snacks to tracks

I feel very fortunate
to know magic is real
and poetry is real
you can see it in the writing if
a belief in one is missing

a mouse eating
the dead
cat our
longed-for
malfunction

I was born
in Topeka
otherwise
they would have
never let me in

they circle away holding this place
opening opening opening OPENING UP
I grope the tree down its root

if truth soothes
soothing was
not truth's goal

my goal
is to do what
produces
memory
as gentle
as vicious
can

one promise: when
I get to the bottom I'll
accelerate deeper
my small pile
of poems
surprising
everyone along the
open wound

"was there a
death" they ask
"a merger" I say

everyone paying attention
enjoy your visit
everyone else
good luck

Aphrodisios

—FOR ERICA KAUFMAN

Wash a penny, rinse it, slip it under your tongue and walk out the door. Copper is the metal of Aphrodite, never ever forget this, never, don't forget it, ever. Drink a little orange juice outside and let some of the juice rest in your mouth with the penny. Oranges are the fruit of Aphrodite, and she is the goddess of Love, but not fidelity. Go somewhere, go, get going with your penny and juice. Where do you want to sit? Find it, and sit there.

What is the best Love you've ever had in this world? Be quiet while thinking about that Love. If someone comes along and starts talking, quietly shoo them away, you're busy, you're a poet with a penny in your mouth, idle chitchat is not your friend. Be quiet so quiet, let the very sounds of that Love be heard in your bones. After a little while take the penny out of your mouth and place it on the top of your head. Balance it there and sit still a little while, for you are now moving your own forces quietly about in your stillness. Now get your pen and paper and write about POVERTY, write line after line about starvation and deprivation from the voice of one who has been Loved in this world.

SHOVEL GIVES IN TO ITS NAME

*Shopping without money is a
challenge with the cameras.*
— MY MOTHER

why are you trembling dear one
my president has come to free you

hair flying at
bullet's impact
the shooter's beautiful
crooked teeth

argued up the evolution of
borrowed faces to
angle potent

my pregnancy dream told me
not born but evicted

length mopped over later
operating a forgotten bell

Venus stipulates a
freedom not to be dismissed or
every grip weakens
smell it to
see it
a joint groans inside its
flesh casing

"have sent it
inside" means
thinking deeper on it as
other waves
proceed through

we cannot train
ourselves to feel less

a silent
misuse of the ordinary until this
moment cannot stand
on its own

each failed attention
sent stinking
pulling your ass apart in
your sleep

no beverage
eliminates the
hunger
ask our
kicked open
bartender as we
bend from
the ceiling with
a fresh ocean-catch
aftertaste

watch through a
hollowed-out bone our

perfection of
brutality as
efficiency

suddenly lacking
courage to
steal every
day's larder

emptying pockets slower
does not bring us to a
new sense of
where we left off

aggravate over our
dumb scratch
the dead can
I promise you

Feast of the Seven Colors

—FOR MAGDALENA ZURAWSKI

Eat a single color of food each day for 7 days, eating through the spectrum our optic nerves are able to decipher: RED, ORANGE, YELLOW, GREEN, BLUE, PURPLE, and WHITE. PURPLE being the transformative, natural pivotal color that is born ONLY WHEN the initiating color RED (which is the first sign of the zodiac, Aries, or Original Fire) and the last color BLUE (which is the final sign of the zodiac, Pisces, or Advanced Water) bleed together. Go ahead and use food coloring as it's about EATING the color, not whether or not RED naturally occurs. Water with food coloring, rice, potatoes, you can do it, you can absorb it for the poems.

Wear or SURROUND yourself with the color. For RED I wore a red wig someone threw in the Dumpster behind the beauty academy near my apartment. For ORANGE I drew an orange ladder on my chest with magic marker. For YELLOW I tucked a yellow condom in my left sock. For GREEN I painted my middle fingernails green. For BLUE I listened to Bobby Vinton's song "Blue Velvet" on a continuous loop from 6 a.m. to midnight. For PUR-PLE I wore purple clothespin nipple clamps all day. For WHITE I painted "108" on my forehead with my boyfriend's semen. EACH color EACH day found me anew. This was a visitation with each chakra, moving from the root to the crown. Each day, before eating or drinking the color sit in a chair, feet flat on the floor, and hum a LOW, DEEP HUM. Reach into that day's chakra, RED the root/sex, GREEN the heart, etc. The notes you take will want out naturally. Work with a clear quartz crystal. On the first day, RED, meditate with the quartz on your groin. Each day move the stone UP your body as you investigate the next color and chakra.

distorted torque of FLORA's red

(WRITTEN AFTER EATING ONLY RED FOODS FOR A
DAY WHILE UNDER THE INFLUENCE OF A RED WIG,
RIGHT SIDE IN CURLS, LEFT SIDE STRAIGHT)

the sick
of magic
lining up

line lost
line made
to disappear on impact

Italian Seasoning on
the Chinese food
frightened
him
at first

fading cow not
far from our
dragon-headed
sperm stains

please stop
prying the dramatics of
the sun

a drape
the line
into no
asking makes

you're so hot when
it's your birthday
direct
descendant
of mud

after they
execute you
they won't return you
to your cell because
you no longer
know how
to suffer

cold
tongue a
line of
credit
ends

a line
the leaves
fall through

weak men are
the danger

listening to prove their
　　loyalty against enemies

　　　　　　knuckled
　　　　　　where a
　　　　　　line asks
　　　　　　a line
　　　　　　to cross
　　　　　　against
　　　　　　the light

dear contentious nativity
　　I was never weak
　　merely outnumbered

　　　　　　shaking
　　　　　　tracks
　　　　　　the line
　　　　　　the trains
　　　　　　follow

　　in Philadelphia
our poems constantly
amend the
Constitution

　　my architect says
　　　　I need more than $108 in
　　　　　　the bank to
　　　　　　build the
　　　　　　poetry hotel

my architect
  asks me to
  stop referring
  to him as
my architect

   the line the
   scalpel
   makes

a system of
sparks warms
  cold spaces between
    the toes

   I sign the Christmas card "to
my architect
  your body
  produced a
  child who
  built a school."

a little orange bag believe it or not CAN hold all that remains

(WRITTEN AFTER EATING ONLY ORANGE FOODS FOR
A DAY WHILE UNDER THE INFLUENCE OF AN ORANGE
LADDER DRAWN ON MY CHEST WITH MAGIC MARKER)

we kissed my
singing radio like
this and this

outta your
eyes outta
your eyes I am certain
the muscle of sorrow is finally
overpowered

you cross the
reflection not my life
the angel of death is
cottontail please stop
the screaming

like this
mouse this one soft
trail under my bed

tonight
if you appear again

I'm waking before
walking into your
                        open arms

                        so sick of
                        the dead so
                        sick of the
                        fucking dead

run to the Mexican border of Canada
run to the Mexican border of Iowa
run to the Mexican border of my kitchen
                                four gas burners
                                already lit

                cumming on painkillers
                is levitating over
                the ocean

                only those who
                never tried it
disbelieve
                                eventually
                        you don't
                        care who
                disbelieves which is
                        the point of
                        painkillers

                suicide's not
understood through

the dictionary any
more than
applesauce

and I'm scared of
shitting orange
but it's inevitable

catching
piano wire
here in
the mouth my
mouth won't
close so sick of this
shit so sick of this crossed-out heart

yelling our
singing we're
fucking and
yelling our reaching around the waist

I'm proud of your
damp crotch in the
cookie aisle hungry from
falling away from remembering
we're a *country at war*

is it time to become unreasonable?
yes it's time to become unreasonable!

let's
demand
nutrient-rich
bullets to nourish
worms made
robust and
prosperous on our
endless
American
shame

the time has come for unreasonable

fuck health care
let's demand magic goldfish with
therapeutic kisses

cross out your own
heart before they arrive

yes
it is
time we serve unreasonable

we're on the brink of UTTER
befuddlement yellow hankie style

(WRITTEN AFTER EATING ONLY YELLOW FOODS
FOR A DAY WHILE UNDER THE INFLUENCE OF A
YELLOW CONDOM TUCKED INTO MY LEFT SOCK)

we never
    think to
    euthanize
    the jockey

ghost of a
    species
      crawling from
    a human
    stampede

not so nice
having the
same hue
    as ham

    I don't
Love you anymore

    there,
now stop asking

glitter
anchors an
eye underskilled for
death

light
the
sperm carries
can engine a
board of
directors
dancers
turn to for
direction

too much
gravity for
a haven I mean
a heaven

two
lungs one
liver
astronauts are
people too
but
you won't believe

something
might hinder this
emphasis of
ferocity

not so safe
bleeding the
same red
as pig

our heavy
metal roots are
never resting
plow blades

you admit
a hard-on while
shooting deer

arrows
and
Eros
same
damn
deal

kissing eliminates
fusion of
agitation and
dreams

folded in the
days these
surprising
moments
with you

                    look under
                     pain and
                          find me
of course I
still
Love you I'm
glad you asked

                     put on your
                hunting
                     boots and
                    look at my
                    antlers I'm a
                    deer I'm
                    a deer!

say it with grEEn paint for the
comfort and healing of their wounds

(WRITTEN AFTER EATING ONLY GREEN FOODS
FOR A DAY WHILE UNDER THE INFLUENCE OF
GREEN NAIL POLISH ON MY MIDDLE FINGERS)

"not until we're
all protected" he said

"not until we're
all unprotected" I said

descent of
magnets we
come
to
bank ourselves against

the tomb
radiates
life without
pause

yes
that's your insurance
agent overhead in
first class

cash webs form
water sends
instinct home

a switch
inside the
queen's body
stops producing
workers to
send out a
queen

the babysitter of
empire wants a raise

write on
walls write on court
house sidewalks write on
every single mirror you
can find
"I MAKE
HOLES IN AFGHAN
FAMILIES EVERY TIME
I PAY MY TAXES!"

all these
centuries later the
occupation
still
u

n

                              w
                           i
                        t tingly
                           shapes the
                              resistance

                        eruptions
                        at night we
                        only hear to
                        know

                           burying
                              dead batteries
                        under the
                        green flag of the
                        desert

                        it's all
                        quite stunning
                        sealed under
                        reactions

                  everybody needs a lover in wartime
                  fuck for the dead
                  fuck and Love fucking for the dead
                  after the latest body count fuck and
                  fuck and fuck the prayer of fucking

                        run
                        onto
                        the

street
screaming Death DOWN!

terrible vacancies
for either
hand

settle into
missing
time flat on
the grass
smoking
hash until the
butterfly

Hyperapathy
I'm telling you this only once
you're
outside
your
jurisdiction

rehab saved his life but drugs
saved mine at the blue HOUR

(WRITTEN AFTER EATING ONLY BLUE FOODS
FOR A DAY WHILE UNDER THE INFLUENCE OF
BOBBY VINTON'S "BLUE VELVET" PLAYED ON A
CONTINUOUS LOOP FROM 6 A.M. TO MIDNIGHT)

as melting glaciers
rush over your
body
what geology?

confused for one
second by your approaching
outstretched
arms

we will the heat
from
toe to hip
fragrance of lightning

world
smells nice today
our semen
dirty ashtrays
well of your armpit
defrosted moss tree leaves are

now buds blue or reflections of
sky smell 11th St. bakery

Philadelphia use
me to get the
Love understood
I'm all yours!

another temperature of
human is
another
folded wing missed by
the tailor

does uranium
smell like
yellow cake?
rust? hot
metal? so many
things I want
to smell but am
not allowed
Franz Kafka's
crotch

new
voice cracks
on a cord of
oxygen when your
finger's
up my ass

I'm not afraid of
my insanity
just my
growing
inability
to hide it

Alice Notley was
not
married to
Ted Hughes stop
talking like
that around me fear makes
every   thing
taste better

your
forgiveness has gotten
expensive
let's pan
expansive
layering
of
fog

press
these halves away
from each other

press
into loosened
air

tentacle suction not
counted on near
the grave

I must stop
carrying my
cave across
the street

dirt on
dark sweaters
hides in the
dark age

we are sons or
daughters
or

smells of summer crotch smells
of new car's purple MAjestY

(WRITTEN AFTER EATING ONLY PURPLE FOODS
FOR A DAY WHILE UNDER THE INFLUENCE
OF PURPLE CLOTHESPIN NIPPLE CLAMPS)

every
day needs an
urgent whistle blown
into it

Thomas Paine's
body
was lost because in
the end no
one
deserved it

he came to
protect us with his
condoms especially the
purple ones *there was*
extra protection

reality is case sensitive for
the poor
keep trying we
keep trying I want to but

am not
there when
I'm there

and
spill it
before they
ask me
not to spill it

I follow my despair
despite
warnings where their
safety obsesses
I am
going INTO it
GOING into IT

in my country it
is legal to purchase
items people suffered
to produce

how long have we
planned for this failure?

coffin manufacturing
perfected to
step up production with a single
phone call reading a headline

                        falling away from
                the gun until
        fighting to
stay awake
        hesitation sometimes
                brings the Love

                        just look for the
                                sharpest thing
                                        in the
                                room my mother
                                        instructed

                        facing certain
                        annihilation he
                        financed his
                        sperm's will to
                        find the egg

                        to panic a
                                panic only
                sex and pot
                        can put at ease

        my neighbor
                killed himself where
        my new neighbor
undresses every morning for
                        her shower

50

it's easier to
fail you and
say I Love you
Cain and Abel
were both to blame
parables pawing the
air with stupidity

it is
much
easier to
fail me
and say you
Love me

X is not blameless

X is not a missed peak

sell these
X pieces for
mouthing off toward
engines of war or
any old halo against
itself

51

from the womb not the anus
WHITE asbestos snowfall on 911

(WRITTEN AFTER EATING ONLY WHITE FOODS FOR
A DAY WHILE UNDER THE INFLUENCE OF "108"
WRITTEN ON MY FOREHEAD WITH FRESH SEMEN)

it's a dog
my heart

my war hair
gets the dead
tangled express message
sent to meet
the approaching
fist

wince
but
do not
burn
away

from more
than one
thing and
more than
one day
Apathy

break from
room where
electricity
hums for
years

retrieve
mind from
socket and
tingly
crotch that
created this
world

does having the
ear of
angels
impress?

but
I would
rather speak
to you

Dear Admiral White Pants
thanks for
the field
guide to
extinct
animals

you make me the
belly who
birds push
through *at last*

the rich can
hire a dominatrix
my mother could
only afford to
marry badly

everything you
know and
do not
know can
be yanked
apart no matter
who you
can
afford

post
traumatic
stress the
grass
bleeding
chlorophyll

do you
like your
fluids to
travel together?

tell me please
about
the calm you
seek when
war is
over

my uncle sneered to
say *what a horrible*
soldier you
would make!
nicest
thing
anyone's ever
said
of me

a dove
lands but
I say nothing
no spell
broken

DOUBLE-shelter

—FOR JOSHUA BECKMAN

thriving requires more than just survival. —ERICA KAUFMAN

If you're preparing to visit someone far away, first spend time studying everyday structures of your own apartment. Where and HOW does the light hit walls? Press your ear to the refrigerator, taste the water with small sips, eyes open, eyes closed. Study the smell and temperature of rooms. Feel your pulse on the toilet, in the shower, by the oven. Cook broccoli with a little oil and salt. Eat it slowly.

As soon as you arrive at the house you are visiting cook broccoli with a little oil and salt. Eat it slowly. Do everything in reverse order, pressing your ear to the refrigerator. How is it different? Take notes while investigating THE TRUTH if there is truth. What does it mean to say THE TRUTH? What matters most? The water has what differences? Are they subtle? Metallic?

Listen to Philip Glass on the floor, on your back, very still, in, the, dark, just, you, and, Mr. Glass. I chose the song "MUSIC IN CONTRARY MOTION." Reflect on a personal violence you want undone. Some terrible THING that removed the beauty you once lived with. My boyfriend Mark (nicknamed Earth) moved to a queer community in Tennessee to work the land. He meditated in a cave each day where homophobic men followed him, bound and gagged him, covered him with gasoline, and set him on fire. For a long time I would go to sleep and dream of stabbing his murderers, shooting his murderers, drowning, choking, and bludgeoning his murderers. Breathtaking dreams of retribution for the man I loved, which, woke, me, each, morning, more inconsolable than the last. I was never going to feel happy again it seemed. Take notes about how the violence in your life will not leave. How it may never leave. Take notes about how you are sensing the world differently since then.

EXPRESS AN INTEREST IN LISTENING
OR FLOWERS WON'T BOTHER

greed it
seems
has no
memory

the little
bones they
throw us
break
my heart

some
days
i taste
the world
in a poem and
want
to be of
service
to that
taste

there is no doubt
the worst possible
things are possible

an epic
terrain of
anger no one
can move
out of you

it's best to let
flowers do
the talking

they say *write*
below your
century to
understand it

they say *crying*
in private helps
no one

they say *touch*
a gill of light
down there

they say *an*
asterisk is
the footnote
to a lie

they say *never*
use "permanent"
in a sentence

containing
a noun

they say *if*
dancing is
prohibited
LEAVE
at once

your BANANA WORD MACHINE

(This is primarily for poets living outside tropical regions.) LOCK THE DOOR AND UNPLUG THE PHONE, KILL all outside interference, you must NOT be interrupted because YOU are about to build and ignite your BANANA WORD MACHINE, and once it gets started it doesn't like to stop, for anyone, for any reason! You need: a banana, and pictures of: parrots, boa constrictors, leopards, jaguars, banana trees, men and women carrying bananas to trucks for export, OR anything else that has to do with banana production, or wildlife or anything else native to where bananas grow. No music. No noise. If there is noise use earplugs. Strip naked and sit on the floor with your pictures, your banana, pen and paper.

Smell the unpeeled banana while looking at each of the pictures you have chosen to build your BANANA WORD MACHINE. When you settle on your favorite picture slowly open the banana, staring at the picture. Imagine this picture ALIVE at the moment it was taken and BE THERE, slowly opening the banana skin, smelling, taking small tastes. When you have absorbed the picture thoroughly, and feel sufficiently transported mentally, get comfortable on your back, then slowly rub banana into your skin wherever you most want to, but make certain to coat your solar plexus, throat, and THOROUGHLY coat your forehead. Feet, genitals, ass, and wherever else you most want to of course since this is YOUR OWN PERSONAL BANANA WORD MACHINE!

Slowly chew a little of the banana, and put the skin on your chest as you stretch out on your back with your eyes closed and FILL YOUR BODY with the LOWEST possible HUM you can muster! SUSTAIN THAT HUM! Then relax in your quiet, hum again, keeping eyes closed. Slowly chew a little more, smell, then just relax in your BRAND-NEW BANANA WORD MACHINE! When you feel quiet, and your muscles quite limber, slowly massage the banana into your forehead, slowly, softly at first, then deeper and

FASTER in a circular, clockwise motion. THEN SUDDENLY SIT UP inside your BANANA WORD MACHINE and write write write write write WRITE! HUM and massage your forehead again to keep your BANANA WORD MACHINE fully in gear and energized! Write, hum, massage, relax, repeat, repeat, keep going, keep going, you, are, writing, in, your BANANA WORD MACHINE! You will write some of the BEST poems of your life TODAY! *YOUR BANANA WORD MACHINE!* *LOVE YOUR BANANA WORD MACHINE!* Yellow splendor!

THE DAY AFTER BEING CENSORED
I REMEMBER MY GRANDMOTHER
SAYING PATIENCE IS THE
HONEST MAN'S REVENGE

lie to your
doctor the
lie will
be treated

caduceus
hot from
misuse

middle is a place
they strive for
the mediocre

in that
and this
town

your town
too and then
the friends
with real
Love come by
this world and
that one the
same skin

milled vibrancy
mulled sensuality

     a perfunctory
     wind knocks
     the third eye at
     a moment some
     call perfect

 between you
and me there

     were wild
     orchids from
     distant jungles
     some birds still
     look for

AZTEC TRYPTOPHAN, REPEAT

—FOR NICOLE DONNELLY & ELEANOR GOUDIE-AVERILL

Eat a little dark chocolate before getting on the subway. Sit in the middle of the car, and don't get on a car where there are no seats for you. Sitting is best for this. Eat a little more dark chocolate. For the next few stops examine the interior of the car with care. Then close your eyes, and as the car rolls on its tracks make a low hum from deep inside you. Don't worry, no one can hear you, trust me, I've tested this with a friend. As soon as the car stops write 9 words as fast as you can before the train moves again. These are not words you were thinking about, just write, don't question what you write, just write. Repeat this humming and writing for 9 stops.

Now get off the train and eat more chocolate. Find a bench or patch of grass. Look at that first set of 9 words carefully, then write something about the words. What do they mean to you? Then move on to the next set of 9 words and repeat. After this is finished, poke around the writing and see what kind of poem is hiding inside it. It's there, trust me it's there. You've just emerged from the underground, rumbling over tracks, and there is something waiting for you to discover it. Please note: Try to not engage with anyone while in the car, or while leaving the subway. Don't break your concentration. Maybe have a little note prepared to hand a friend you might run into which explains why you can't talk to them. Don't wait for their response, just hand them the note and get about your business, you're busy. And they will understand, don't worry, just get going for your poem.

The Sun God's Daughter
Has a Lovely Copper Penis

if I had a pussy
I suppose I'd know
what to do with it

why does she
laugh at his stupid
jokes I know she
knows his jokes
are stupid I'm
exhausted for her

pen stabbing this out
these vines
tasted sunlight
before I tasted
their blossoms
pen trying
for that
2nd hand
sunny
flavor

what a rare and
beautiful blood
type you are

throwing life to it
throws your life to it
throw me, our

falling
backwards is a
new love of mine

against the crack to hold the light back

what about
Passover? Oh
a hangover well
that's better

because I don't have
a pussy is no excuse but
let me say something
completely different now

Chuck Norris needs
his own candy bar
one with big nuts
what are those big
nuts called?
yeah some of those
I would eat one
every day
make that
twice a day
is it possible

to make a candy bar
with warm nougat
maybe have
it shoot out
well we need to
work on that
call it
Big Norris 'N Nuts
or maybe
Chuck In the Mouth
yeah that works
Chuck In the Mouth
oh my god it's
so delicious and
it doesn't even
exist
yet
half the proceeds
should go to
gay pride parades
where gay people
don't even live
everyone needs a gay pride parade
hire professional gay pride marchers
this is silly you say
but I told you I was going to
say something completely different

YOU IN YOUR SOUP

—FOR JULIANA SPAHR & DAVID BUUCK

First we must gather ingredients for the soup. Whatever you want, but my soup included: carrots, onions, beets, burdock root, celery, kale, mustard greens, chard (4 roots, 4 stalks & greens, or an even exchange with yang underground and yin aboveground), salt and water. Before chopping, sit with all the ingredients in your lap, or at least near you while you meditate however it is you meditate. But try to meditate on how this FOOD SOURCE is about to become your body. Chop and cook your soup. After the soup has cooled, pour it in a deep bowl, deep enough that you can submerge your hand.

Unplug the phone, ignore the world. If you are right-handed then your left hand will be submerged in the soup, or the reverse, if the reverse. Sit for a while with eyes closed. FEEL-ING the soup with the submerged hand, pinch bits of carrot, or whatever is in there, FEEL it FEEL it, feel IT before IT'S eaten. Take notes about your body and the soup in the bowl before it becomes your body. The roots have recently been HUMMING underground forging themselves, stalks and leaves stretching into the light, and rain, and slight flutter of insect wings, ALL have now COOKED TOGETHER to become YOU. Take notes, take notes, many notes.

Use a HUGE spoon if you have one, this to reduce your sense of your own size. Take notes about what IT MEANS TO YOU to reduce your sense of your own size. Dip the spoon into the soup, scraping your hand, eat. Take notes about how this tastes, take notes about YOUR marinated hand soup. Are the ingredients organic? Take notes, take notes, source of THE SOURCE is for the notes now. If ingredients are not organic, were there labels at the store telling where they were from? Take notes. Were any ingredients GMO? How do you feel about GMO foods? Notes, notes. Cup your submerged hand and eat from it. Run your tongue along the surface of your hand, and lick your fingers clean. Put your hand back in your soup. Can you feel the soup in your body, in your blood, coursing through you, can you feel this yet? Eat your soup with your HUGE spoon and cupped hand eat it eat it eat it all, licking the bowl and licking your hand CLEAN. Take notes about ANYTHING that comes to mind, pressing your now SOUPLESS hand to your forehead thinking thinking thinking about ANYTHING at all running your now SOUPLESS hand ALL OVER YOUR HEAD while thinking and writing.

KICK THE FLUSH

when I die I want the blue
lights in my head to
come on when I
wake tomorrow I want the
blue lights to disappear
it's not extinction
it's a new bloom who
weeds can grow up with
a marvelous
understatement opening miles
we never counted how many
dents we made in
HIS head we just wanted
the giant unconscious
we wanted safety
we were too frightened to
fucking count
we're driving away
faster, then faster and faster
no one needs
to know how many
dents we put in HIS head
give me over listless to a
grass-filled mote
whose seismic odor
gives me up easy as
anyone some days
it's the impossibility of

innocence pleasing this
gonad plantation but it
ain't coming up through me
bonus-ing out the systems with
a fade-away sentence of
the sun
keep your threats at
blade-level so THEY
see we mean it
this is not a fucking
joke you dirty pothead
death hurts faster when flying
the giant
held us to the
light to
squint at our
translucent qualities
we were never traded cold
we were wild by the inches
we were always HIS favorite
as my smell of memory insists
HE could if HE
wanted to develop
an odor to please us take
HIS shirt off
aid our anticipation
but when HE demanded respect HE
was surprised to
find out what HE
really deserved
the problem with

giants is THEY believe
THEIR mothers
THEY imbibe tears of
suffering flowers
we grab umbrellas
gravitate toward
a past vantage of water
"planes is how WE hear the sky" the
idiot giant would tell us
it was HIS need to
apologize that drove HIM
to uploading
rude sensations
HIS fracture of listening
causing whistle blanks
that's when
we woke the blue
lights in HIS head
it's how we earned our freedom
now I open my gorgeous entrails to
the sun
let birds circle with
watering mouths
sew myself up before
they land
teasing birds with my
beautiful guts my
lifelong dream fulfilled

TAPPING FLESH FOR SAP

—FOR DOROTHEA LASKY & THOM DONOVAN

This exercise needs 9 consecutive days. Take 9 books of poetry by LIVING POETS ONLY, but choose books of poetry you turn to again and again. Choose the order of the books for the 9 days, then place an oak leaf (preferably late spring leaf) in the first book. Sleep with the book under your pillow. Next day take the oak leaf from the book and bite a chunk off and keep it in your mouth. Find a recording of wolves howling, or even a recording you made yourself of friends howling. But if you make the recording, direct your friends to a Rallying Howl, then a Defensive Howl; let them decide what that means.

Listen to the recording on headphones and go outside chewing your leaf, keeping the book on you, in a bag, under your arm, between your ass cheeks, it's up to you. Walk where there are people, walk where you can find THE MOST people. Keep chewing with the howling while studying faces and arms, studying how people move with one another, move around one another. Take notes, take as many notes as you can. When you're tired of chewing your leaf move it between your teeth and gums, but don't spit: swallow, don't spit. Remember that this leaf has been soaked in the book while you were dreaming. This isn't about appropriating text, it's about text absorption, the leaf taking on vibratory elements. Take notes about how the leaf tastes while thinking about how the book made you feel the first time you read it.

SUDDENLY look up and find someone you are sure would howl a howl you would recognize as one of your tribe, your pack. Take notes about them-to-you in your world. Repeat this exercise for the 9 days, a different book each day, the same leaf though, it's important to keep the same leaf, the leaf building layers of absorption. Now take all your notes from the 9 days to make either one poem from all the notes, or 9 different poems, it's up to you.

ONE

LEAF PRESSED IN *NEGATIVITY*
BY JOCELYN SAIDENBERG

need to find a
          hinge on something
          anything need to
          feel its hinge exertions
          (closed eyes feel closer)

TWO

LEAF PRESSED IN *SOME NOTES ON MY PROGRAMMING* BY ANSELM BERRIGAN

the history of art
is not the future *(what a relief)*
          this is private property they say
so is this middle finger I say naked in
a bucket of water digesting the room

THREE

LEAF PRESSED IN *DISASTER SUITES* BY ROB HALPERN

I washed
but they smell my kill
undeniable excitement for bounty finds a place to gasp
it's a gasping room there's
gasping all day here

FOUR

LEAF PRESSED IN *POLLEN MEMORY*
BY LAYNIE BROWNE

we will be majestic within
this hour as well as
the next   blending
sequential motives to align
fang with fist

FIVE

LEAF PRESSED IN *THINGS OF EACH POSSIBLE RELATION HASHING AGAINST ONE ANOTHER* BY JULIANA SPAHR

years of starvation
paved freedom to
fit finally between
metal and
porcelain barricades

SIX

LEAF PRESSED IN *ON MY WAY* BY EILEEN MYLES

trained to locate
grocery stores *(architecture confused for real estate)*
eating's only a
matter of time
after the purchase

SEVEN

LEAF PRESSED IN *DEED* BY ROD SMITH

with devotional care
with magnanimous care
we
become the brand we
will buy

EIGHT

LEAF PRESSED IN *CENSORY IMPULSE*
BY ERICA KAUFMAN

cocaine my cocaine friend
lines connecting
our fabled exhaust makes us
elastic makes us sensual injuries
makes us catalysts for spinning the room

NINE

confectioner killers breast-feeding our

exhilarated battle for

organs of the rehabilitated

lamb

bestow his liver and heart upon the bride and groom

RADIANT ELVIS MRI

—FOR THE PSYCHIC LEGACY OF HANNAH WEINER

Don't be afraid of the MRI (Magnetic Resonance Imaging) machine, it's an amazing opportunity for a poem. I created this exercise after my knee was injured by a homophobic bus driver in Philadelphia. Astral travel is possible with some dedicated preparation. The MRI machine needs our water molecules in our bodies for the imaging process, the electromagnetic field literally shifting the alignment of the protons of our body-water. Drink only crystal-infused water for a week before your MRI, drink no other water, and drink it as often as you can. Look at the label for "silica" content. It's important to saturate the body with as much crystal water as possible leading up to the day of the MRI.

Choose a place you will visit for your psychic or astral visit (a room in your home for instance). For the week leading up to your MRI, each time you enter your chosen space STOP at the entrance, and take a long look around. Then close your eyes and imagine what you saw. Open your eyes and notice what you missed when imagining what you saw, for it is the missing things you will incorporate each time you repeat this exercise until you have gathered the entire space in your mind. The space I chose is a street in Philadelphia, a place I know more than any other place on our planet. For years I have been gathering the minute details of this one stretch of street: gutters, glass, bricks, trees, newspaper boxes, all the many details. Every time I walk to this street I prepare myself to STOP and drink it in, and notice something new to add to this growing landscape in my mind.

On the day of your MRI sit and listen to music by Elvis Presley for an hour or so. Elvis Presley is being used ALL OVER OUR PLANET for healing. When I wrote my book *Advanced Elvis Course* there were many people I met who use Elvis to heal bodies and spirits, and when you listen to Elvis you tap into that collective use of His powers. The song I listened to on repeat before my MRI was "I Got a Feeling in My Body," with the refrain, "I got a feeling in my body / This will be our lucky day / We'll be releasing all our sorrow / Leave it layin' along the way." Elvis assists in setting the crystal-infused water molecules right for the MRI machine. Take many notes all week long leading up to your RADIANT ELVIS MRI.

Depending on the type of scan that is needed you may have as much as half an hour in the machine, *and this is good!* Let yourself relax for a few minutes. Take some deep breaths. When the pulse of the machine amps up and begins to shift the alignment of your crystal-laden water molecules SEE the space you have been memorizing for the past week. SEE IT. Look at all the details you have been studying. The longer you keep inside this space the quicker and easier you will GO THERE. Go, and don't be afraid to leave your body behind you to do so. Make yourself sit, stand, jump, float, BE in that space in all ways. Find words if you can, like Hannah Weiner found on foreheads, look for words to remember. You'll know how to come back, don't worry yourself. Make sure you have a notebook ready to write in as soon as you get out of the machine. Leave the office and find a place to sit and take notes about your experience for your poem.

separation is natural SHAKE WELL

it's a relief when
strangers die
love's an arduous loss
I saw my friend's
turd in the toilet
I was amazed and
looked closely to see
the hard work as
amazing as my own our
blood and muscles at the
mercy of food to survive
that's a good-looking turd
vitamins absorbed by my
friend's healthy body
the turd discard floating
we eat apples for
violent nutrient extraction
it's a beautiful day
apple trees everywhere
drinking light with leaves
drinking water with roots
I will stand quietly in
the orchard while the
farmer sprays barrels
of pesticide
this is a violence as
delicious as I
choose to make it if

I'm going to have
my planet and
eat it too
it's rude saying
pterodactyls are
extinct their molecules
eaten by something to be
eaten by something to be
eaten by us
at noon tomorrow
let's squeeze
our nipples to
remember our
pterodactyl flesh

your CRYSTAL GRID

—FOR MELISSA BUZZEO

Do you have a favorite gemstone? Are you familiar with its geological history, its mythology and healing properties? There are amethyst, rose quartz, emerald, ruby, hematite, garnet, tiger's eye, and hundreds of others. Once you have a stone you want to work with, and have educated yourself about its assets and particular characteristics, take a sheet of blank white paper and draw a map of the streets or roads surrounding your home. Once your map is drawn, sit very quietly with your stone, the map in front of you. Close your eyes and meditate on the healing properties and other legends pertaining to your stone. When you feel ready, open your eyes AND WITHOUT THINKING throw the stone onto the map.

Now go to that location with the stone. When you arrive drink in the landscape. Be quiet, be invisible. Stand there, or sit there and be quiet, the stone in your hand. In your notebook take notes about what you see, feel, hear, smell, take it all in and write it all down. Then IMAGINE how the properties of your stone FIT into the world before you. For instance, if you hold amethyst, the purple color is from iron impurities within the stone, and it's valued for treating the nervous system and is said to strengthen memory functions, which accounts for its lore as being a stone of wisdom. It is known as a gemstone of peace, and is a good source of psychic protection, warding off deception and calming the bearer. These are things if you used amethyst you would consider when incorporating the stone's properties into the landscape where the map led you. Take notes, take many notes bringing your stone into the physical surroundings, and note how your stone helps you better examine the world.

Signal and Sway

everything

    vibrates

and we

get to

    feel

con

cen

tration has

the Love

saying Magic without

embarrassment

i fail the

end of

suffering

with you

boots

bought ten years

ago by

younger man

same name

every

vibrating

thing

bared
teeth ahead
visible
for
some
time

an invitation
to the fist

so adorable
trembling
for
predators

excuse me
i meant to
say *fuck you*

knives coming
down
trying
to eat it

is it the
emotional distance
of the waitress
you come for?

aria of snail
ticking smaller

in the sound
breathing louder
in the light

how long
can we believe
this world
belongs to us?

is it a
toilet or
grave being
made?

he answers
by asking
is it a cartoon
or fiction?

BETWEEN CORRESPONDING WAVES

—FOR JOCELYN SAIDENBERG & ROB HALPERN

Gather sand from the Atlantic and Pacific Oceans. When I collected sand in Atlantic City I meditated with the ocean for an hour, then dug a hole, placed a quartz crystal in the hole, covered it with sand and crystal-infused water. I repeated this ritual at Ocean Beach in San Francisco. During both rituals I was conscious of facing AWAY from America. East and AWAY! West and AWAY! Migration of senses, their capacities perceived and pursued.

Back home, using a compass, I positioned the head of my bed north for 4 nights of concentrated ocean dream enhancement. Night 1: Atlantic sand in a cloth under my pillow with a continuous recording of ocean tides playing from the east. I drank crystal-infused water to better remember my dreams. As soon as I woke I took my notes DO NOT DO ANYTHING PEE CRY ANSWER THE PHONE MAKE LOVE until you have taken your notes. Night 2: Repeat ritual, except use Pacific sand in a fresh cloth under the pillow and play ocean tides from the west. Night 3: Repeat ritual, except have both cloths of sand under the pillow and play ocean tides from east and west. As you begin to doze, listen for when the tides match pace, your body between them, America between them. Night 4: Mix the sand in a fresh cloth for the pillow, then play ocean tides from east, west, north, and south. Set the alarm to wake in the middle of the night, move your head south, sand now at your feet in the north. Gather your 4 rounds of notes and sculpt your poem.

AMERICA YOU DON'T GIVE A DAMN ABOUT THEIR DEAD

if your soul were
wood would you
invite termites?

dream of bombing

a living moment
living a moment

my favorite weather
is what it is

more

dreaming

of bombs finding
the line

slowly look at
photograph of
busy people

finding the line the
defining line

Baghdad
I forgot you
died and called
your house

bombs igniting a line against our dreaming
you answered
our dream you
don't want to
vanish you
don't want
to vanish I
understand
I understand: THERE IS
NO SOLUTION but to be
the line the bombs follow

ARISE IN YOUR DROSS!

—FOR ISH KLEIN WHO SEES ART IN GARBAGE

SAVE YOUR garbage for a week, every wrapper, every box, carton, save it all. Rinse it out if you must, but it's better if you don't, better to SMELL it. At the end of the week go through each item, slowly, carefully, do it in a closed room, don't let anyone bother you. Don't answer the door or the phone, IGNORE THEM, you're busy looking at garbage to build a poem! Take some notes, write down interesting facts from labels, or the size of things, how they look, how you remember them at the cash register. Imagine where this packaging came from, factories, and before that fields and trucks and many many hands picking, cutting, grinding, printing with color and black ink. Take notes when thinking about these things. SMELL them one at a time with eyes closed, eyes opened, eyes closed again SMELLING, deeply SMELLING. Notes, take your notes.

NOW GET NAKED AND GET IN THE BATHTUB, and go underwater, blow bubbles. Go under again and stay under a little longer. DO THIS several more times then COME UP, dry your hands on the side of the tub and grab your notes, and WRITE about drowning, pull your notes together to write a poem about drowning and YOU'RE ABOUT TO DIE drowning BUT THIS IS what you want to share at the end. GO BACK UNDER the water again, then COME UP AGAIN and WRITE!

RANCOR COLLECTS ME BY THE THROAT

the best funeral
I've ever been to
was the night we intended to
cope with this Love
the increase is beautiful
like poems by a poet who
finally gave up on fear
every chance every dog
everywhere
ever gets
my mother's okay with it
I caught her having
sex with my
babysitter Marcy she yelled S H E ' S
G O T   A   T O N G U E   D O E S N ' T   S H E
odd and strange when
marriage and military make
your favorite M words
every time every eye
every door
ever blackened
being a hijacker
not a stowaway
my mother arrested for
stealing a jar of honey
but who will arrest the
thieves of bees there is
no permission there

is no permission THERE IS
NO PERMISSION there is
only death and the
life you live or
are led by

OIL THIS WAR!

—FOR JONATHAN SKINNER

How is it where you live? If there are no wealthy people and/or the poor are nurtured and protected, then maybe this exercise is not for you? I have been littering in wealthy neighborhoods with JOYFUL PROTEST for some time now! It is exciting to SEE "refuse" in the open, not hidden in landfills, if only for a moment. Here in Philadelphia taxes pay for uniformed workers to clean prosperous neighborhoods of cigarette butts, cans, and wrappers all day, each day, while completely ignoring working-class and poor communities. Philadelphia public school students have a 51 percent dropout rate, and 25 percent of the city's population lives below the poverty line (that's 1 in 4 people THAT'S 1 IN 4 PEOPLE!). The police patrol and protect the rich while they INFAMOUSLY threaten, beat, and rob the poor (just ask *Philadelphia Daily News* reporters Barbara Laker & Wendy Ruderman). WE MUST RESIST! WE MUST BE RESISTANCE! Take initial notes on the class structure of where you live.

Save your "garbage" for a week, packaging and containers, especially plastics. Take notes about each item, tracing its origin of production from label information or the manufacturer's website. Find other companies they work with; for instance a candy bar needs chocolate from South America, and plastics, inks, and glue for wrappers. Trace on a map the distance each item needs to travel to the candy bar factory, then from the factory to your city. Calculate gasoline and oil consumption per mile. And consider that plastics are petroleum by-products. And not just the packaging, but in fact many goods themselves are made from oil: hand lotion, shoes, ballpoint pens, disposable diapers, glue, rubbing alcohol, soda and milk jugs, credit cards, nail polish, ink, crayons, and more. Much of the modern world IS oil. Toys, televisions, telephones, microchips, luggage, cars, condoms—it's in the air, water, soil, food, IT'S IN OUR BODIES! Take notes about oil, take notes about your discovery of oil consumption in ways you had never considered or realized. After immersing yourself in this information STOP! Then write nonstop for 30 minutes, WHATEVER comes to mind, just write! Let it flow! THIS is when the best language for our poems will arise!

Real change needs creativity and action! Using a black marker write suggestive notes on your "garbage." Littering in wealthy neighborhoods is precarious but gratifying! Just IMAGINE them reading your used tampon marked US WAR! and puzzling over the message. Make the rich THINK! Or at least make their children think! OIL OIL EVERYWHERE! Write on old shoes, sandwich wrappers, cans, bags, snotty tissues, used condoms, THIS OIL WAR! On an empty bottle of hand lotion OIL THIS WAR! On a cereal box THIS FAGGOT WORLD VICTORIOUS! On a soda bottle YOUR SISSY CHIL- DREN SAVE THE WORLD FROM YOU! As citizens it is our duty to communi- cate the temperature of SUFFERING! Littering helps us SEE our planet's transmuted el- ements before they're swept into trucks and hauled to the dump, far, far away, leaking toxins into the water and soil. A tidy sidewalk does NOT EQUAL thoughtful, mindful citizenry! CITIZENS OF THE WORLD RISE UP AND FILL THE STREETS OF THE AFFLUENT WITH YOUR SHIT AND "GARBAGE" TODAY! Let them SMELL and READ the products of THEIR WARS! Write on your "garbage," WE DEMAND A PLANET SAFE FOR ANIMALS AND OTHER HU- MANS! Take notes about your littering excursions. Take notes about the neighborhoods you visit with your deposits. Take notes, take MANY notes, then STOP! Write for 30 minutes on autopilot. Always remember to carry your notes with you wherever you go to pull and wrench your poem into existence.

Duck Call for Dead Ducks

with daffodil center
he walks like he's
never tasted
his own cum

a window for
dangling
mentors above
their death

UNFAIRRRR
screamed
back up the
building

the more
inequitable the
more potent
the smell

there will
be their
will to
consider

planting
watering nurturing
dead seeds without
knowing it

tip of
cigarette
reworks
the table

trees we
did not cut
a kind of
legacy

MUGGED into poetry

If you haven't been stabbed or shot, if they took your money under threat and left, consider a poem. After I was mugged recently in Philadelphia this exercise came to mind on the subway ride home, the postmugging subway ride when poetry took its rightful place at the center of my world where even muggers play a part in it, it being bigger than the knife, more concentrated and firmer than his cock which will have many admirers in prison. He's going to die. So am I. So are you. He could have EASILY killed me, he and his three friends BUT I AM ALIVE AND QUITE WELL writing for poetry as I willingly came to this cesspool of humanity to do. All the globe becomes a poem. It is enough to manage this small part, here, a body, in a body, stinking, beautiful, a bit of tormented, angry, tender, delicious flesh. It is enough. Each of us. If we can read this we are all alive and creative. Anyone who tells you that you are not creative is a coward afraid of his own potential, trust me. Ignore all cowards, they were born to be ignored. Find your strength, find your poems.

Every morning for 2 weeks as soon as you waken PREDICT your death. And write it down. For instance, "by choking in 11 years, 4 months, 2 weeks, 6 days, 12:18 p.m." THEN STARTING at the tips of your toes touch your cells of skin and nails, feel bones, your pulse, hair, feel your moving body in the morning ALWAYS moving as long as you live you are moving blood through veins moving thoughts through dreams EVERY morning for 2 weeks touch every inch of your body's surface and your holes moist and dry. As soon as you finish this reaffirming ritual write a poem from your moving blood in the thoughts of the dream, and combine that LIVING poem with the prediction of your death.

1

by choking in
11 years
4 months
2 weeks
6 days
12:18 p.m.

———

when i win the lottery
i want my legs amputated
and two beautiful peg legs
wooden of course

Frank Sherlock says it's
a very bad idea
he says i should
reconsider
seriously
reconsider

i want peg legs but
he says i'll regret it
he might be right

but what i really
want is to have my
real legs (the ones
i don't want)
cremated because
what i really want
is to scatter
my own
ashes

i thought about getting
liposuction and having
the fat cremated
but it's not
the same
because i can
eat more
delicious
doughnuts and
grow it back

it doesn't count

it HAS to be
something
missing for
good you
know

but to
spread my

own ashes is something
i love thinking about
and the cheerful
sound of my
peg legs on
Philadelphia
sidewalks

2

by tornado in
16 years
5 months
2 weeks
6 days
8:49 a.m.

———

i'm trying
to make the
tree ring
i mean this
you know what
i mean
exactly yes
i'm trying

to make the

tree ring

it's fortunate

more leaves

don't cover

us in the

process i'm

open to abstraction

on this page a

painting

literally

more

abstraction lost in copious design

some of the orange

signs tell us

exactly how

you go if you

drive or abstract

winnings of

extractable

longitudes

looters display

winning contents

on the

mattress a

winning

collage

things

you

use

are

losing the
way to get
at trying to
make the
tree ring
an effort an
effort you
say an effort
but you say you also say
mayonnaise does it better
so then mayonnaise it

3

by bludgeoning in
4 years
10 months
1 week
1 day
6:22 a.m.

———

MY FIRST AFGHAN MEAL WAS WITH
FRANK SHERLOCK AND RON SILLIMAN
THREE YEARS AFTER THE AMERICAN
INVASION OF AFGHANISTAN

delicious
turnover how
many people
were killed
that day?
the waitress was nice
was the music Afghan?
no, Egyptian
i don't understand
Kandahar or the
Korengal Valley any
more than i do
Valley Forge
and i've been
to Valley Forge
a lot
the
deer and
daisies are
not why it's
remembered
and if the
battles had
not been
waged
those hills
would have
been part
of King of
Prussia
shopping

mall

the

importance

of war kept this soil free from a

legion of

cement

trucks and

steel

National Park

National Park the

cannon and

the cannon

and the

cannon

ball

tree

roots

cradle

4

by stroke in

39 years

11 months

3 weeks

6 days

8:19 p.m.

―――

FYI

your 45-minute
talk felt like
3 hours
i'm not a big
fan of similes
but it was
like listening to
Hedda Gabler
describe a
dental hygiene exam and after the first
hour and a half of
your 45 minutes
i prayed for
the angel of
death to break
through the
ceiling and
snatch me
away

by falling off a radio tower in
8 years
4 months
1 week
6 days
3:42 a.m.

———

(what i'm about to say is not
nostalgia for, or a sentimental
reunion for, but a painful need
for agreeing that
we're not crazy)

Some
Times i want
To visit the
Locations
Of the three
UFOs i've
Seen with
Friends

Brooklyn, New York with
Frank Sherlock

Chinatown, Philadelphia with
Elizabeth Angelo

Cornwall, England with
Jo Mariner

6

by nuclear missile in
2 years
2 months
3 weeks
6 days
9:47 a.m.

———

i convinced my
sometimes-boyfriend
Peanut to swallow
a beautiful quartz
gemstone

it came to me to
have it pass through
Peanut's body
then

clean it
swallow it myself

this special stone's
specialness increased
from passing
through
our bodies

it will vibrate of
our shared
pregnancy

two men in
love three
times a week
sometimes
four times

7

by falling into an elevator shaft in
6 years
4 months
2 weeks
5 days
midnight

dream of frying giant leaves with christina strong at her new home in hawaii pink little pink (NEON PINK) butterflies fly out of the leaves as we cook them she says it's a good sign i ask her if she's sure she says while waving a freshly lit joint NEVER DOUBT A BUT-TERFLY CONRAD!

second part of dream i fly into NY from hawaii and Christina meets me at airport we take subway into town there are advertisements for lockheed martin on train i say CHRISTINA THERE ARE ADS FOR LOCKHEED MARTIN she says I KNOW I KNOW i asked WHY THOUGH WHY ON EARTH she says WHILE YOU WERE AWAY WAR ENDED AND NOW THEY NEED TO ADVERTISE BECAUSE OF WORLD PEACE it was the most exciting news ever we got off at 2nd Ave and there were thousands of people hugging in the streets

(some dreams like this dream i want to reenact exactly)

8

by electrocution in
4 years
11 months
1 week
1 day
4:13 a.m.

i really
love moving
while
standing still
sitting still
i do it by
escalator
bus
airplane
elevator
horse
car
train
trolley
LSD

(must admit most of
my acid trips have
been evil i need
a lighter trip
diet LSD)

9

by wild dogs in
14 years
7 months

3 weeks
2 days
1:00 a.m.

———

there were four of them it was the strangest mugging i was going to a poetry reading in philadelphia walked the wrong way they called out from behind me as if they knew me the one with the knife came around first "AW, HEY, HE'S A DUDE!" a little confused by my long hair bright green shirt purple glitter nail polish two were behind me while another faced me and asked
"are you gay?"
"yes"
"my cousin is gay"
"do you like your cousin?"
"yeah, my cousin's cool, i LOVE my family"
while the one with the knife pointed at my heart then my stomach jerking in his hand pointed at my head then my groin he was irritated by our conversation "JUST GIVE ME YOUR WALLET MAN!" he found only twelve dollars "TWELVE DOLLARS IS ALL YOU GOT!?" the one who likes his gay cousin said "just take the cash, cards are hard to replace" they argued but took only the cash dropped the wallet ran off three dollars for each of them but it was a gay-positive mugging

10

by lung cancer in
12 years
8 months

2 weeks

6 days

4:17 p.m.

———

GATHER HIS SPERM! someone must dress as a nurse (I'LL DO IT!) cheerfully walk into Dick Cheney's hospital room (I'LL DO IT!) jerk him off into a dixie cup (I'LL DO IT!) seed-gathering magic spell for the future demon caste (I'LL DO IT!) "This is your happy ending Demon Cheney, hope you enjoy!"

11

by drowning in

13 years

3 months

2 weeks

6 days

4:12 p.m.

———

DICK CHENEY is so close to death today i can smell his funeral flowers MMM SO DELICIOUS i want to eat Dick's pretty little posy wosy!

1 2

by heart attack in

50 years

4 months

3 weeks

6 days

2:15 p.m.

———

dream of making a GIANT CAKE in Penny Arcade's apartment we are laughing because marshmallows when baked become tiny people but if you bake them too long it kills them we keep checking to make sure we aren't killing tiny marshmallow people we bring them out they stand on our hands singing Penny says while laughing WHAT AM I GOING TO DO WITH THEM ALL? i say EAT THEM! then they run away to hide in the apartment we crack up laughing again of course

1 3

by stabbing in

10 years

2 months

1 week

4 days

3:15 a.m.

—

these anxieties
will themselves
to fit my
aching
head

then
suddenly
HEAR pain
give ground

1 4

by car wreck in
23 years
4 months
6 days
noon

—

woke to
idling
truck

a willing
earthling
interested in
award-winning
seat belts

XX

a little note at the end of this series of poems:

i'm going to have
a samosa-eating
contest with
myself but before
i do oh people
of the future
i am so angry
that you walk
beautiful with life
my city's streets
without me after
i die but go to
my favorite
corner please
and wave at
the sky please

22nd & Chestnut Streets,
Philadelphia,
Pennsylvania,
United States of America,
Planet Earth,
Milky Way Galaxy,
the Universe

A BEAUTIFUL
MARSUPIAL
AFTERNOON

Someone downtown bought a new refrigerator and I carried the large cardboard box upstairs to my apartment. Lined with blankets and pillows it was the perfect marsupial pouch for the new poetry exercise. I punched a hole in the back and inserted a baby bottle filled with soy milk to suck on. Just outside the box DVDs of Pasolini's films played, first *The Decameron*, then *The Canterbury Tales*. An entire world of human sexual intrigue and treachery outside, my, warm, pouch, here, I, am. HOW do I make the world comfortable every day I ask myself? HOW do I manage to get up in the morning KNOWING that my taxes pay for bullets and bombs to kill the people of Iraq and Afghanistan? In 2009 three children died every single day in Afghanistan from war-related injuries. HOW did I not kill myself with worry and guilt? HOW often do I think about being complicit in the degradation of life on Earth?

My boyfriend came over, we played Pasolini's *SALÒ OR THE 120 DAYS OF SODOM*. We removed the baby bottle from the back of my cardboard pouch and my boyfriend used it as a glory hole. Graffiti around his cock AND THEN little wigs for its head made of cotton and pillow stuffing. I glued a frame around the hole, asked him to back up and enter again slower, slowly, a portrait of a cannon at the castle gates maybe? YES! Finding the spaces between hating this world, finding and loving those spaces. Today. Tomorrow. It's going to become a poem from the pouch. My cardboard MOMMA, Pasolini, and the glory hole of a beautiful marsupial afternoon. Thanks to you who make things delicious and wonderful. Without you despair would appreciate its earnings. Notes from this day are to become a poem.

RESEMBLANCE DEPRECIATION

America I am America
and I'm telling myself
STOP IT NOW!

on a garbage
can mouth a
THANK YOU

Fire Island did
not float away
it's in the state
of New York in the
United States it's
there it's still
there they called
and checked
it's where
Frank O'Hara
was killed

I'm afraid
of the photograph

blood in sand
his killer
lived with it
he didn't mean it
he read the complete
poems and art
reviews after the funeral

what a stupid night to
make you read poetry mister

THANK YOU on garbage can
"it's lying" he thinks
you're right mister
nobody's going to
thank you go
fuck yourself you
fucking poet killer

America I am America
I'm not going to
tell you again
if I can't reveal
to you I will
revel instead

I'm going to
stop calling this
our world it's not
our world because
something else is
ready to show us
it's not and
it's moving in
close now it's
close my god
we fucked up

A Nude in a BUCKET

—FOR JASON ZUZGA

In your home alone, take a bucket or basin of room-temperature water to your front door and strip naked. Put a piece of paper or thin notepad under the bucket and lay a pen nearby. Stand in the water. Get used to being naked while standing in water at the front door. Look through the peephole. Look for a long time at the world out there. Then look above you, and at the door, the walls, and make note of something you hadn't seen before—maybe a cobweb or crack in the paint. Every once in a while stretch your arms over your head stretch as high as you can stretch stretch stretch then relax in your bucket. If someone knocks or rings the bell it's your good fortune! Look at them through the peephole while saying nothing. Maybe have a friend come over at a certain time to knock and say, "Are you naked in your bucket of water?" Don't answer, you're a poet, this isn't time for idle chitchat, besides that you can warn them ahead of time that you won't be answering. Stretch, and be quiet. Step out of the bucket and sit your poet ass on the floor, get the paper from under the bucket and whistle short, loud bursts of whistle 4 times. Then write. When you feel the need for more whistles, pause, whistle, then write some more.

Shiva's Four Hands Kneading
the Dough That Is Your Face

descent of butter

eaten by a man pushed from

a cliff

ammunition

amnesia

amnesty

in order of

appearance in dictionary

unless you purge them

jealous poets will cut you into

the headlong

shadow

of metal

piercing shadow

of flesh

I was on the

chair when he sucked the

room into himself

smells of

shit in here! walls of shit-smell!

four quiet days later my growing chant
nature regulate us!
nature regulate us!
NATURE REGULATE US!

encroaching desert of kari's last blog
post

guard larynx from tension of lies
from forces of hardening
from those the Muses abandon

believe me
you'll believe the
green when it's gone

ambition for candy
ambition for industry
ambition for immortality
even ambition to have no ambition

time scales our
blankets unimpressed

wildly opened
damage disperses
the creeps

dreamer pressed
against other dreamers
hooks

softly
clanging

we lose
our way back but
spirit feels
home

serial number written on
a balloon a
white balloon gone
after a few minutes
over
rooftops

TOUCH YOURSELF FOR ART

—FOR PENNY ARCADE

There must be a piece of art near where you live that you enjoy, even LOVE! A piece of art that IF THERE WAS WAR you would steal it and hide it in your little apartment. I'm going to PACK my apartment TO THE ROOF when war comes! This exercise needs 7 days, but not 7 consecutive days as most museums and galleries are not open 7 days a week. At the Philadelphia Museum of Art hangs the Mark Rothko "Orange, Red and Yellow, 1961" a painting I would marry and cherish in sickness and in health, have its little Rothko babies, and hang them on the wall with their father. But I'm not allowed to even touch it! The security guards will think you're as weird as they think I am when you come for 7 days to sit and meditate. Never mind that, bribe them with candy, cigarettes or soda, whatever it takes to be left in peace. For 7 days I sat with my dearest Rothko.

Bring binoculars because you will get closer to the painting than anyone else in the room! Feel free to fall in love with what you see, you're a poet, you're writing a poem, go ahead and fall in love! Feel free to go to the museum restroom and touch yourself in the stall, and be sure to write on the wall that you were there and what you were doing as everyone enjoys a dedication to details in the museum. And be certain to leave your number, you never know what other art lover will be reading. Return with your binoculars. There is no museum in the world with rules against the use of binoculars, information you may need for the guards if you run out of cigarettes and candy.

Map your 7 days with physical treats to enhance your experience: mint leaves to suck, chocolate liqueurs, cotton balls between your toes, firm-fitting satin underwear, things you can rock-out with in secret for the art you love. Take notes, there must be a concentration on notes in your pleasure making. Never mind how horrifying your notes may become, horror and pleasure have an illogical mix when you touch yourself for art. When you gather your 7 days of notes you will see the poem waiting in there. Pull it out like pulling yourself out of a long and energizing dream.

ROTHKO7

Whether things wither or whether your ability to see them does.
—from "The Coinciding," by CARRIE HUNTER

DAY 1

it's
October
I pressed
this buttercup in April
I DON'T CARE WHAT YOU THINK
call me it!
call me sentimental!
HAVE YOU SEEN THE HEADLINES?
spring is a
luxury
I hope
for another to
garden with my
bare hands

DAY2

<pre>
awkwardness of being insane
                  arrives
                    after
                diagnosis
              not before
remove description
from the splendor
do not hesitate
</pre>

DAY3

<pre>
     more of a ghost
   than my ghosts
     here I am
</pre>

DAY4

tablet on tongue
stray voltage catching
my ankles

ready to marry
the chopped
off head

while elaborate in curse
it contributes evidence
of life

DAY5

he kissed me while
I sang
refrain shoved
against epiglottis

centuries of a vowel for
endless refutable corrections
puts mouth
to want

songs dying bodies sing at
             involuntary
             junctures of
                   living

             EXIT sign
         leads us to empty
             launch pad
             walking
             maybe
             walking
             maybe or riding
         the collapsing tower

             big hands of
             big clock missing
     this is not symbolism
             they were gone

DAY7

I'm not tearing back
curtains looking
I know Love is
on the other
side of
town

burying the leash
with the dog was
nothing but
cruel don't ever
speak to me again
help me stop
dreaming your
destruction

your Zoe Magnifier

What is your favorite Zoe Strauss photograph? Everyone has one, or two, or many. For this exercise get your copy of her book *AMERICA* and find one. "STAY ALIVE" is a favorite of mine. What is your favorite canned vegetable? I love canned peas. Canned peas would make a lovely pillow in a coffin or dream. Think about your favorite canned vegetable in your life, take notes. This exercise needs 3 consecutive nights.

1: BOILED canned peas, very simple, careful to carry the scent and texture through the mouth, sinuses, and let's be CHEWING while looking carefully at Zoe's photograph. Eyes open WIDE, look through a hole in the bottom of a box. ALLOW ALL MIXTURE of senses to explore. Take notes then go to bed. When you wake, what dreams did you have?

2: FRIED canned peas, in olive oil, a little toothpick to eat them one at a time while looking at Zoe's photograph with a magnifying glass, then through pantyhose. The clouds in "STAY ALIVE" move over the trees in my dreams. One night my old boyfriend Tommy who died of AIDS was in Zoe's photograph, standing near the yellow sign along the highway, its black letters commanding "STAY ALIVE." He pointed to it, "Did you read this today?"

3: FROZEN canned peas, spread out with salt on wax paper in the freezer, QUITE DELICIOUS! Tonight stare at one part of the photograph, STARE without blinking for as long as you can. Then pop a delicious frozen pea in your mouth and close your eyes. SEE the details of the photograph in your mind. Open your eyes, focus on another detail of the photograph, then pop another delicious frozen pea in your mouth. Close your eyes and THIS TIME imagine someone you love thawing from ice as the pea warms on your tongue. How are they doing? What do you like most about this photograph? Pop another frozen pea, keep your eyes OPEN, but shut the light off, then back on, off, on again, over and over, all the while popping delicious frozen peas. EYES WIDE OPEN in light, in dark, seeing, chewing, then suddenly STOP in the dark. Let your eyes adjust to the darkness, the photograph taking shape in the shadows around it. Staring at the unlit photograph look for MOVEMENT and take notes about what you see. Dreams this night are for more notes the next morning. All the notes from this exercise will come together into a poem.

hours inside philaDELPHIa

—FOR ZOE STRAUSS

serenade leading
to a bloody
condom

between
these words
a resting
hammer
between
these letters
a scaffold
trembling in
its rust

even the average
crime begs a
little glory

i'm not so
pretty with
my skin
removed

no he said
prettier

STUDY FOR SHOPPING
MALL TREES

—FOR EILEEN MYLES

Go to a shopping mall parking lot with trees and other landscaping growing between the parked cars to create this poem. Find a tree you connect with, feel it out, bark, branches, leaves. Sit on its roots to see if it wants you OFF! These trees are SICK WITH converting car exhaust and shopper exhale all fucking day! Sit with your tree friend. Don't pay attention to the cars coming in and out of the parking lot, you're here to write poetry, not to worry about what a lunatic you appear to be. Remember what our QUEEN poet of merging celestial bodies Mina Loy said, "If you are very frank with yourself and don't mind how ridiculous anything that comes to you may seem, you will have a chance of capturing the symbol of your direct reaction."

Public space is not easy in shopping mall parking lots, but calmly explain yourself to the security guards as I did when creating this exercise. They will train a camera on you, but the sooner you get rid of them the sooner you can train the camera of your brain. Take notes, feverishly at first. These initial notes will help rid you of any concerns of respectability. Use a magnifying glass to study the dirt, trunk, to look carefully at leaf veins and bark structure. Notes, take notes, writing quickly, as if you've just discovered a sleeping creature that may wake at any moment and ATTACK YOU! Smell your hand, smell a branch. Study then the sky and buildings and people and everything, every detail.

Face one direction and stare for a few seconds. Close your eyes and while they're closed imagine what you saw. Open your eyes and notice what you missed when imagining what you saw. Study what was missed and where and how it exists near your tree friend. Take notes. If you are right-handed then touch the tree with your left hand, for your left hand is the hand that absorbs the world. Then walk to other trees in the parking lot and touch them with your right hand, for your right hand is the hand that sends your messages OUT of you. Touching your right hand to the other trees sends OUT of you the message your tree friend put into you through your left hand. Take notes on what was said from tree to tree. What message were you carrying? Take notes while leaving. Later, at home, close your eyes and remember your tree friend, take more notes from this visit with your memory.

SHOPPING MALL TREES

hypnotized before the slaughter

                                many
            prefer trees as baseball bats
            porch swings
                                cellos
                                    violins
                    trees dead on stage
                    orchestra of singing dead

                no one
                no matter how powerful
                king martyr executioner
                    can kill a tree twice
                    smashing violin
            torching cello touching ash to
                            nipple suck
                                suck
                            sucky thy milk

                                we need
        a joy to signal the way backward from no music

    to hear absolute magic as absolutely natural

        suppose we see it come undone
            unbristled unalarmed
            finally unalarmed

all private parts at the melting winter

sex with trees   an
                    involuntary
musculature of Love open to stillness
pussy-syrup saliva semen branch sap leaf

surrender or not
                    fragmentation remains

crinkle of passing car stereo alludes to
a million private thoughts
an entire imagined room roped in its hemisphere
                              remembering
                    every
              pillow
slept on
knowing some are missing

ANTENNA JIVE

—FOR BEN MALKIN

Find a small tree, prepare the ground with blankets for you and your partner on either side of the tree. Get undressed, completely, get on your blanket, your partner facing you. Have the flats of your feet pressed together, the tree in between your pairs of legs. Both of you rest on your backs, and press your feet, press them with legs raised, then lowered. For a little while work together in this meditation of pressing and moving legs and feet with the tree quietly growing between them. Take notes about how you're feeling.

Make it clear ahead of time that he or she working with you is free to do, say, sing whatever they want, so long as you keep the bottoms of your feet connected around the tree. My boyfriend Rich did this with me, singing, humming, and finally masturbating, sitting up and smearing his semen on the bark. His orgasm PUSHED our feet together at a critical moment of note taking for me, good for my note taking. Let this (Soma)tic Exercise have as much freedom for the two of you as possible, the frequency given and taken and shared with the tree between you, a living antenna between you, pulling nutrients from the earth and sun rays. The tree between us is where the notes came most clearly for me. WHATEVER YOU DO please do not give any additional instructions to your partner, let THEM do EXACTLY what they want to do once you're both on the ground naked together with the tree between you. THEIR freedom to express themselves depends upon this poem as much as your feet pressing together around the tree. But take notes, take many many notes.

AN EXORCISM FOR THE HELL OF IT

we are laughing
we are in this room laughing
    now and a glass or two
      I WILL NOT THINK OF YOU DEAD
      I WILL NOT THINK OF YOU DEAD
      (mantra against too much loss)

        tonight the myth of healing will allow
the machine of sleep to make us on
           the other side

our new minerals
new technologies will rise to meet

    towns collecting on the
     mapmaker's desk a coffee stain or
mountain range lights swept into the valley as if
miracles wander too close to the door

             cut walls until
              no criminal
              can hide

          who will prevent our
          knowing stability of
          a new holdout?

organize a slipping tone of gray
arrange a landing for a thousand
models of loneliness

something fits a
situated darkness despite the
whimpering "no"

starved of patience
taste of release

only in the brightest day we find two
colonies of ants battling under a tree
we learned from them my god
we learned from them
YOU ARE BEAUTIFUL ANTS
STOP FIGHTING!

AIDS SNOW FAMILY

—FOR ANYONE WHO LOVED SOMEONE WHO DIED OF AIDS

The poem is restorative, rather than fragmenting. —ALEXANDRA GRILIKHES

In January gather snow; this is intimate, this calling to honor the shock of being alive. I made one tiny snowman named CAConrad, and one tiny snowman named Tommy Schneider. For six months they held hands in the privacy of my freezer while I visited the streets and buildings in the Philadelphia of our Love. Snow crystals travel miles out of clouds into the light of our city. My snowman read to his snowman the letters I brought home to the freezer. It's 2010, AIDS is different in this century you didn't live to see. The used bookshop where you worked on South Street is now a clothing store. Our first kiss in the Poetry section is a rack of blue jeans and I resist hooking my thumbs in the belt loops to pull you in—I FEEL you everywhere today.

In March an old friend was visiting and she said, "But you wrote poems for Tommy after he died." I said, "But it's sublime retracing our Love in this exercise." She shook her head, "No, it's sad, it's very sad. Can't you see this beautiful day?" OF COURSE I see the beautiful day, in fact I SEE IT MORE THAN EVER, and I don't need her choreography to enter it. The point of experiencing Love is to engage the greater openings. It's important to ignore the directives of others when investigating the way these doors swing on their hinges. Months of spring into summer, my snowman told your snowman the memories. One night you had asked if I was upset at something. I said, "I have no right to complain, all the men are dying in our city and I don't have AIDS!" You said, "Well I have no right to complain because I have a wonderful boyfriend who loves me and I DO have AIDS!"

Macrobiotics, herbal infusions, massages, sensory deprivation tanks, reflexology, music by Soft Cell, music by Siouxsie and the Banshees, music by Cocteau Twins, music by Patti

Smith. Of course we're all dying, you'll never kiss someone who isn't dying, I know that, which is why the fear of this is not allowed to stop me from missing you the way I want. The streets were filled with men in wheelchairs that year. We were kids in love while you vanished in the funnel with them. The day after Summer Solstice I took our snowmen out of the freezer. 90 degrees, we melted quicker than expected, even sooner than I could have imagined. I burned the letters, mixed their ash with our slush. And I read to the puddle a poem that came to me years ago in a dream soon after you died: *he wrote "I have AIDS / and kissed this wall" / X marked the spot / I wrote "I'm not afraid" / and kissed him back / wherever he is.* I took many notes during the life of our snowmen in the freezer until they vanished. Those notes became a poem.

QUALM CUTTING

AND ASSEMBLAGE

—FOR TOMMY SCHNEIDER

What do you think
of the cosmic
proletariat?
—DEBRAH MORKUN

deshrouded

against

a ton of

ears a five

pound

song

broke

them all

it is

rare to

remember

where we

are from

listen

I am on

earth

not sure

how long

our documents

under rubble
an hour
prying this
fucking
drawer
open to
find handles
and screws
instead of
your poem
we came into
the quiet like
we had to
survive their
ridicule
to die
in their
sleeping
conscience
bleeding
as when
bathed in
the hunt
you fund
me with
kisses
face a
spoken
promise
the written
has been

burned
only a
memory
can perish
every
cell
resold to
sharpest
set of
incisors
"viruses are
hungry too"
you said
our documents
shot into
outer space
what is
more fortunate
than the
will to
proceed
bliss
cascading
in the
candy you
make as
a sword
gathers
me into
solitude
cradling

a five
pound
song for
you in
my ear
I hate many
but won't halt
loving you
set this
down to know
a little night
time
heads, macaroni
tails, execution
edit our bigger
part of credit
the cop
Frank O'Hara
not the poet
Frank O'Hara
told us
STOP
GETTING
NAKED
IN THE
BUSHES
TOGETHER
he's gonna have
to arrest us he's
gonna have to
arrest us he's

trying so
hard to
be nice
remembering
half finished
poems falling
off table
falling off
truck falling
off cliff
what's that
fucking cliff
trying to
do to us
this is how
it feels
traffic lights
in dark
in rain
no cars even
pink hat in
sidewalk drain
it's the
comfort
you get
some
times
I molded
my body
around
you to

hold your
winter to a
sanctum of
flame
we agree
to ignore
the
deafening
knock
lingering at
dollhouse
doors
large
sentimental
songs at
dollhouse
doors
dolls yelling
FUCK OFF
an anger
traces the
outline of
each it
enters
it is
and is
not a private
act to involve the
thawing choir
our bones
our muscles

get rising
to one
and
two
breaths
the common
lung this
world a
mouth into
a mouth
breathing
back
and
forth
so
then
so
then
mouth
sings to
mouth
so then
mouth
sings to
mouth
so then
all night
so then
a day
then a
day so

POETRY is DIRT as
DEATH is DIRT

—FOR DAVID WOLACH

Go to your local graveyard, spend some time searching for a spot to sit. Be where no one will bother you, you're busy, you're here to write poetry, not to be pestered with small talk! When you have found your place sit on the ground. Take time to look closely at ALL OBJECTS at your feet, in the trees, etc. Find 3 objects, one of them on the ground, or at least touching the ground: your feet, a grave marker, tree trunk or roots, etc. The other 2 off the ground in a tree, a building, but make them things that are stationary so you can stay focused on them. Draw a triangle connecting these 3 objects. Focus hard on the contents of your triangle, keeping in mind that the ground object you have chosen connects to the dead.

Imagine your triangle in different forms of light, weather, and seasons. Imagine someone you love in the triangle dying. Imagine yourself inside it dying. Gather notes in this process, take notes, as many notes as you can about how you feel and what you feel. Then PAUSE from these notes to focus again on your triangle, THEN write QUICKLY AND WITH-OUT THINKING for as much time as you can manage. Often it's these spontaneous notes that dislodge important information for us. DO NOT HESITATE to write the most brutal things that come to mind, HESITATE at nothing for that matter. Take some deep breaths and think about death by murder, war, cancer, suicide, accidents, knives, fire, drowning, crushing, decapitation, torture, plagues, animal attacks, dehydration, guns, stones, tanks, bombs, genocide, strokes, explosions, electrocutions, guillotine, firing squads, parasites, suffocation, flash floods, tornadoes, earthquakes, cyanide, poison, capital punishment, falling, stampedes, strangulation, freezing, baseball bats, overdose, plane crashes, fist fights, choking, etc., imagine every possible form of death. Take notes on your feelings for death at this point, DO NOT HESITATE.

I'm TOO Lazy for this World

I went to the very

Real bank with

A gun for the

Fiction of

Money

A beautiful poem should

Help you rob a bank

That's its job

Everything has a job

Can we get

through this without yelling wait

WAIT you are already

Angry it's too much

you must get as tired

as I do

I'm never using the gun again

I'm too lazy for your wars

we could cancel this back from the basement

no more rifle no more M16 last

time flesh split in dreams for

months muscles rip hear that

muscle rip it's too much here's a

glass of water let's get through

this okay maybe not maybe it's

time to admit we can't do it

millions of years slashing into

one another

my gentle living

against what is meant to perform

I'm too lazy to kill

three children a day

Lieutenant Sergeant

US MARINE CORPS YES SIR

my Buddhist friend tries calming

his urge to butcher it's possible

some days it seems possible

what about today how do we feel

about not snuffing animals and

other people today what about

today one day without killing it

feels possible but

I'm new at problem

solving without the

gallows what do you

say I mean there are

so many I would LOVE to see

swinging by their necks they

deserve it they do they really do I

see them I see them I see them

swinging swinging SWINGING

some days I want to be nice I

really do but so many are

swinging by their necks in these

dreams some days I would tie the

noose myself JUST TO PROVE

they deserve it I don't care I DO

NOT care but sometimes I do

care I do I do care I do want to

care believe me it is not how you
will question me when you order
me to the ankle-deep sentence of
the concluding measure of the
way in which we live
order me to see if I will obey you I'm not sure
I can listen go ahead and try, oh, okay so I
didn't listen that is all I can tell you is that you
can't order me but it was worth a try how can
we administer another button to the whole
project one that pushes and stays pushed
when I'm surprised I like to answer myself in
code it rushes back and forth the way I open
up to the thing whatever the thing is hold this
soda and ask me to nicely forget the way we
met it's the only way to interrupt the former
solutions okay oh okay so it didn't work either
I'm tired of poetry not
saving the world
forgetting its job
give me the map where absolute silence
determines our placement
order me
order me up
make us indeterminate
or else there is no
position for the wind
to capsize us please hurry
this is a mess and I need to engage
you where it catches the lip of your coat
everyone's Beware of Dog signs
fences walls crossing property lines

the LAST GREAT transgression I
break into your house make rice in
your kitchen then offer you a taste why
are you screaming I should leave you
will call the police you're such an
asshole calling them this is just an
experiment in erasing ownership you
coward you fiend you make me wish
murder was legal get one person a
year NO NOT JUST one a lifetime or
the rich would buy our murder-rations
depriving us of the joys of murder how
to be nice today take it one day then
another not killing
not doing it no no no
we absolute the sentence in
the making of fortune

please don't kill not today just
one day let them live just today
we'll try again tomorrow

there's no murder-ration card to
hand the police I should leave
your kitchen maybe we could be
friends okay you have enough
friends stop screaming I get it I
get it you have property it is paid
for all the taxes all the wages
streaming out your fucking
windows you are a bounty of
opportunity with more than
enough friends

CONFETTI ALLEGIANCE

Is there a deceased poet who was alive in your lifetime but you never met, and you wish you had met? A poet you would LOVE to correspond with, but it's too late? Take notes about this missed opportunity. What is your favorite poem by this poet? Write it on unlined paper by hand (no typing). If we were gods we wouldn't need to invent beautiful poems, and that's why our lives are more interesting, and that's why the gods are always meddling in our affairs out of boredom. It's like the fascination the rich have with the poor. As Alice Notley says, "The poor are more interesting than others, almost uniformly." This poem was written by a human poet, and we humans love our poets, if we have any sense. Does something strike flint in you from the process of engaging your body to write this poem you know and love? Notes, notes, take notes.

The poet for me in doing this exercise is Jim Brodey and his poem "Little Light," which he wrote in the bathtub while listening to the music of Eric Dolphy, masturbating in the middle of the poem, "while the soot-tinted noise of too-full streets echoes / and I pick up the quietly diminishing soap *& do* / myself again." Take your handwritten version of the poem and cut it into tiny confetti. Heat olive oil in a frying pan and toss the confetti poem in. Add garlic, onion, parsnip, whatever you want, pepper it, salt it, serve it over noodles or rice. Eat the delicious poem with a nice glass of red wine, pausing to read it out loud and toast the poet, "MANY APOLOGIES FOR NOT TOASTING YOU WHEN YOU WERE ALIVE!" Take notes while slowly chewing the poem. Chew slowly so your saliva breaks the poem down before it slides into your belly to feed your blood and cells of your body. Gather your notes, write your poem.

LOVE LETTER TO JIM BRODEY

Dear Jim
for
those whose
acid trips were a success
only twice
I've met men who
are high exactly
as they are sober
both became my lovers

both died one like
you died Jim he
played music too
loud at parties to
gather us into a
single frequency feel
healed for the length
of a song

nothing works forever
there was something in
the air that year Jim
and you put it there

a rapt center in
pivot looking
to face
Love again

155

learning to
accept what's offered
without guilt

to be reminded
of nothing
my favorite day not dragging
the dead around

they're looking
for Lorca in the Valley
of the Fallen

Franco's thugs would understand
"developing countries" means
getting them ready for
mining diamonds drilling oil
teaching them to make a
decent cup of coffee for
visiting executives

if I'm not going
to live like this
anymore I must will
every cell to
stand away

the *History of Madness*
725 pages is too much to
not be normal

scorn is very

motivating

                        I'm vegetarian unless
            angels are on the
            menu mouthwatering
            deep-fried wings
            shove greasy bones in
            their trumpets

      the cost of
                  scorn is
                  often unexpected

      I see my fascist
      neighbor from downstairs
      "Did my boyfriend and
      I make too much
      noise last night?"
      his glare the
      YES that keeps
      me smiling

(SOMA)TIC POETICS

an interview with CAConrad

by Thom Donovan

CONDUCTED IN THE SPRING OF 2011

IN PHILADELPHIA AND NEW YORK

Thom Donovan: Conrad. Basically I'm wondering what, if anything, inspired you or gave you the idea to write the (Soma)tic Exercises? What was the germ, in other words, of this beautiful project?

CAConrad: YOU and other friends is an answer. But also war, AIDS, studying macrobiotics, healing herbs, and studying deep-tissue massage. Also my studies of Norse mythology and the runes with Freya Aswynn, and, frankly, a thousand other things coming together to form a large lens, or filter, with which to take a closer examination of life through poetry.

War is a fact we're told to accept. I refuse to acculturate, meaning that mine is a poetics of uncooperation for all the brutal strategies built to sustain capital gain. I insist we make these national tragedies personal. We invaded Baghdad on the spring equinox of 2003, blood libations for the gods of war. On the third anniversary of this invasion I woke DEMANDING of myself that I create some THING in my life to be a constant reminder that we are at war. I thought about hanging a sign in my apartment, but knew it would become ineffective. Then I considered getting a WAR CRIMINAL tattoo because we are war criminals for paying our taxes KNOWING that those taxes buy bullets that kill children overseas. But no, I wanted something constantly changing yet ON me or WITH me at all times. My dead neighbor Owen haunts the building where I live in Philadelphia, I sometimes hear him and feel his presence. That morning when I lay in bed thinking about what I should have in my life to remind me of our nation's atrocities, he whispered in my ear USE YOUR HAIR! Use my hair, HOW brilliant, thank you Owen! I don't cut my hair and it gets longer and LONGER with the war and needs more and MORE care as does the war. Every morning I look my American self in the mirror and ask my hair, FOR EVERY INCH HOW MANY PEOPLE SUFFERED AND DIED? This is an ongoing project of intense hubris, frankly, a very long (Soma)tic love poem for the war-dead through my WAR HAIR. I have manifested physically this mournful disposition, and it's on the top of me, pressing down all the time, and I'm under it trying to find a way to love this world as it is, and to not let it kill me, which is ironic since MY American life kills so many other lives. I've had dreams where my hair is on fire and I don't put it out and it feels good, fire burning into my skull where my thoughts live. I hate my hair and I'm so disappointed that we allow war to continue. Then of course as you know, the United States celebrated the spring equinox of 2011 by bombing Libya, MORE blood for the gods of war! Aries BEGINS on the spring equinox, as we know, and its ruling planet is Mars, big surprise. I DON'T KNOW how long we can put up with being told lies for this killing! Stupidity is the saddest human quality, and I use (Soma)tics willfully, always, with my war hair.

In 2004 Frank Sherlock, Linh Dinh, Mytili Jagannathan, and I formed PACE in Philadelphia, which is an acronym for Poet-Activist Community Extension. PACE is also the Italian word for "peace." We each made a broadside of a poem that confronted the wars in Iraq and Afghanistan, and we then went out to the city streets on Christmas Eve to read these poems for frantic, last-minute shoppers. We were confronting people on the sidewalks with our poems, and of course we didn't know what to expect. What we discovered was that everyone WANTED this, they WANTED these poems, they WANTED to talk candidly about the wars being waged. They wanted to say we were lied to by our leaders. They wanted to share the shame and anger. We were out there suffering together, and, frankly, it felt good, unexpectedly good. It was immensely depressing watching the death toll rise AND RISE and not being able to stop it. Taking our bodies and our poems out to the streets was one of the most powerful acts of community, locating the shared sadness, and the dispirited, overwhelmed resistance.

Another answer to your question is AIDS. When I was a queer kid dealing with violent ridicule in rural Pennsylvania, well, that was hard enough, but then AIDS came along. In other words, I was already terrified of my body because I was queer, but THEN came this disease, which many of my classmates were quick to point out was my own personal disease, a symptom of my perversion. My body became the very center of evil, and I believed them for a little while. Even when I thought I didn't, I did. Recovering from self-hatred is an amazing plan if you can have it.

This sounds strange but being queer made creativity easier for me if only because I was shunned, forced outside the acceptable, respectable world, and writing was something I turned to in that imposed solitude, for writing was an actual place I could go to where I was free. Not an escape by the way! I really HATE when writers say they write to ESCAPE! I escape nothing, ever, nor do I want to escape! But this is my opportunity to say I'm grateful for being queer.

It was also very fortunate for my life and my poetry that I learned about macrobiotics from my friend Jay Pinsky while I was still quite young in Philadelphia. It was macrobiotics where I first learned how we strip nutrients from other living things to feed our cells. THE MOL-ECULES! THE MOLECULES! And eating an animal-free diet of locally grown vegetables was something I could FEEL create a different, cleaner, clearer body and mind almost immediately. It gave me a fresh start, and saved my life and my poems.

For ten years I was solidly macrobiotic, 1988 to 1998. And I remember at the end of the first year eating this vegan diet of local foods, I remember TUNING IN on the world around me in a way I had never imagined was possible. I entered the body of my local world with cellular focus. It startles, that level of awakening, and is exciting with a half-frightening kind of excitement! The dirt, the insects, the way veins in leaves cut space through the surface, suddenly everything had a spectrum of scent and color which had been opaque to me before this time. I tried to get my boyfriend Tommy to become macrobiotic because he had AIDS, and eventually died of it. I loved him very much, it was difficult, and frankly it's still difficult to talk about Tommy. I also worked with ESSIAC, which is an herbal infusion, and this combination of herbalism and macrobiotics led me to the world in a way I had no idea was existing all that time around me without my knowing it. And I'm talking about truly GETTING the interconnectedness, seeing the web of life that we are a part of on this planet, forgoing the simpler Tree of Life model.

But it was this learned compassion for myself, other people and other animals that helped me come to the conclusion that there is a creative viability in everything around us. Before compassion and healing, this fact of everything being rich with the promise of creativity was impossible for me to see. In tandem with macrobiotics I started attending pagan festivals and studying various disciplines of witchcraft. It was through the pagan community that I started to incorporate a political and spiritual practice with my newfound understanding of my body and poetry.

To sum up my answer for you though, I would say my WAR HAIR, and recovering from oppression of my body led me to hear and trust the engine in everything. Every single thing can now be highlighted as a possible WAY to a poem. It's true to say the poem is there, it's right there, it's always there, and it's waiting, actually waiting for us. It's like the poet Alice Notley says, "Poetry's so common hardly anyone can find it." I LOVE that she says that!

(Soma)tics are how I live in my awareness. This is a new word, the "o" a long "o." This word is simultaneously two words: *Soma* and *Somatic*. It's the mutation(s) occurring when these wires cross where the poems can be found. This poetry truly is in everything, underscoring Freud's statement, "Everywhere I go I find a poet has been there before me."

The Institute of Contemporary Art's recent *Queer Voice* show included a (Soma)tic poem that I wrote for the exhibition catalogue. The responsibility I felt at the invitation to write this led me to thinking that if the AIDS crisis has taught me anything it is the necessity of living in this world with fellow travelers. The spaces we fight for today must be the shared spaces, those which exemplify radical inclusivity. My worldview advocates decentralized power structures in economic and political governance, and art can lead the way to societal horizontalism. My first book, *Deviant Propulsion,* is a collection of poems that speak of deviance as a source of courage that pushes boundaries to propel culture forward. Poetry and other art disciplines are forms of courage, and the queer voice belongs to anyone willing to take on that hard work, regardless of how else they identify, beyond being human.

You ask what's at stake though. Well, we're living in a country where we have the first president with African blood, and there are racist white people who are so angry that they ACTUALLY insisted he show them his birth certificate to prove he's American, because they keep thinking that there has to be a loophole to this because they cannot accept this president. There's a kind of madness in the air. And we're also living in a country where if your mother is white and your father is black, you're black. No one ever says, "We have the first biracial president." No, everyone just says he's black. There is this AWFUL bigoted assessment that if you're partially black then you can't claim the white, like the white got dirty and no one wants it. It's really fucking horrible these judgments, but it's built into our language. Not that racism isn't everywhere else in the world, but I need to concern myself with my country, especially now that we're presently in three racist wars at once. In 1835 Alexis de Tocqueville wrote, "The greatness of America lies not in being more enlightened than any other nation, but rather in her ability to repair her faults." In 2011 I'm not so sure we're capable any longer. I'm completely discouraged. How will we ever be able to apologize to the mothers of

Afghanistan? Last year three children died of war-related injuries every single day in their country. EVERY SINGLE DAY. I mean, well I mean what on earth can be done? What? I'm glad Thom you ask what's at stake for bringing (Soma)tics into poetry, because I ask, "What's at stake for NOT bringing it into poetry?" Whenever someone asks what the wars are costing I answer as loud and as obnoxiously as I can, "EVERYTHING!"

And if you've grown up in trauma you know firsthand. I grew up in a house with a pedophile, and let me tell you about that stress. A stress that takes its toll physically as well as mentally. Every day you're thinking about your sister, "Is she home from school before me? I HAVE TO GET HOME before she does!" My days were spent making sure she was never alone with him. When you're a child fending for another child in a world where the adults have become completely useless in their greed and violence, you learn early that our bodies are sensitive living matter. Wanting to protect another's body with your body, yes, and using a gun, yes, getting ready for the ultimate means of protection. And also learning signs of the old man's incredible sexual appetite, which he extinguishes with alcohol and pot. An awareness is necessary. The awareness of the body means everything at such times. Everything will be destroyed if you do not, and you know it. Somatic is the real, breathing life.

Somatic is derived from the Greek, and it's our flesh. It's also the body's cavity, the place where our organs rest, live, and work. The organs where EVERYTHING we eat, drink, and breathe EVERY DAY gets processed, built into the cells of the body, or of course discarded. THE MOLECULES! THE MOLECULES! I like to take the traditional definition of Somatic further because I believe VERY STRONGLY that every memory we have is cellular. The latest research on the human brain locates the actual, physical life of memory. Memory is a THING. It's in the brain, and it's alive, as alive as a toe or lip. We also know from centuries of pressure-point manipulation, acupuncture, and massage that muscles and other human tissue hold memories. Our bodies actually remember. They remember trauma, love, joy. Memory is everything, for without it we couldn't be having this conversation. Living in the present, as my Buddhist friends keep urging, is futile. It's a search that needs the memory of language, the memory of conduct, love, fear; it's a search, which relies, as any search would rely, on memory, and all memory is past unless you are psychic and see the future, but that's just another kind of memory. I have nothing against Buddhism by the way, in fact I have more affection for Buddhism than any other structured religion. My religion is Poetry, not a religion of kindness and love but one of absolute permission. If Poetry doesn't strip me naked in front of my enemies then nothing will.

Soma is from the Indo-Persian, and means "to press and be newly born." In other words psychedelic and energizing plants were pressed—or juiced—together, then consumed, but seeking the divine is the goal. Some people think I use Soma in (Soma)tics for drug use. I don't care who uses drugs, I'm not here to judge, but I'm not interested in drugs these days. Drug use and healing are similar in that they are both seeking altered states, but the altered state I want now is healthier.

What I care about MOST is that the word *Soma* is INSIDE the word *Somatic*, clearly honed for the divine within. It's always been right in front of us, this collusion of hemispheres, and for that you need no drugs. I'm on the edge of my seat every single day, waiting to see what pries me open by meddling with what I consider very inconclusive evidence of the definitions of Somatic and Soma. It's quite beautiful.

(Soma)tic praxis is testing the boundaries of both Soma and Somatic, pushing ourselves to experience new impressions and sensations. In a recent workshop I asked us to spy on a menagerie of dolls on a fireplace mantel, with binoculars, while taking the pulse of the person next to you. Someone doing this said, "This is sensory overload." And it is. Taking the living, thumping pulse of someone while carefully studying a community of dolls animates the moment. Dolls have been used for centuries to represent spirits, even to house spirits.

You mentioned Notley by name before, but do you feel like there are somatic or (Soma)tic poets who precede you in your religious pantheon? If so, who? Can you talk about their somatic practices with regard to your own, also? What, if anything, do you take away from them/their work? How can their work be useful to a contemporary somatic/(Soma)tic writing practice?

Well, first let me say that yes, the first formal (Soma)tic workshop—although there was nothing formal about it—was in 2008, but after the first (Soma)tic poem, the one I deliberately wrote as a (Soma)tic poem in 2005, I began a series of collaborations with others to make (Soma)tic poems. A year later I began growing my WAR HAIR, but that first poem, which became seven poems, was subsequently published as *(Soma)tic Midge*. And I called it "midge" because a midge is a little bug, an insect, and it flies around, buzz buzz annoying. And I knew that THIS was merely the beginning of some THING and some WAY to SEE how poetry is everywhere. It was liberating to finally trust in the world this way. A poet learning TRUST is essential learning. Trusting the world, trusting the audience. When a poet is verbose in the line it's usually a result of their thinking the audience isn't capable without them. They are, they very much are capable, and the sooner we learn it the better for our poems, frankly.

As for other poets who precede me, who have inspired (Soma)tics, this is a long list, but let me make a few clear. A big one is Charles Olson by way of Jonathan Williams. I say by way of Jonathan Williams because one of my FAVORITE things to do when visiting Jonathan was to get him to talk about Olson at Black Mountain. One conversation that had a deep impact on me was Jonathan's describing a class where Olson instructed them to listen to a piece of music by Dvořák, then RUN across an open field to write their poems where the natural light was better. Olson told them the field and sun would be in the poem. To me this statement of Olson's wasn't saying the field and sun should make cameos in the poems. This was instead an acknowledgment that the infinite qualities of our world are inherently THERE; they are ALWAYS IN the poems. There is no such thing as NOTHING. Try for nothing and the very cells of your brain hunting for nothing are themselves something. Olson wasn't merely accepting BUT WELCOMING the interconnectedness of all things to bring forth poems. THIS IS WHY poetry is my religion, because it is the place where we are permitted to sit and gain access to our Soma no matter who we are.

But think about what Olson was instructing at Black Mountain that day. You're listening to Dvořák, and according to Jonathan it was AS LOUD as Olson could get it to be. THEN you RUN across a field of grass, flowers, your body involved AFTER the Dvořák melting down your eardrums, THEN there is this light, the light he asks you to participate WITH, to write the poem IN. Run, you must run, through the light, in the light, AFTER the music settled into your bones. It's marvelous, and became windows for me into the ways experience outside norms force disequilibrium. These states not only garner a momentary new set of awareness for the senses, but also present the possibility of changing the structures of thought for entire new ideas and new practices of forming ideas.

When I was a kid I spent many hours along the highway selling bouquets of flowers for my mother. That forced isolation became time for reading and learning under the cloud of car exhaust. Poverty—believe it or not—gave me the opportunity to SIT STILL AND READ! I remember reading *NADJA* by Breton, and the line "Beauty will be convulsive or not at all" GRABBED ME! Breton instantly made poetry something you taste and smell, TRULY VISCERAL, he brought it to the body. He was saying you have to feel it, actually feel it. I wanted nothing more than to feel it!

When I was fourteen I discovered the poems of Mayakovsky in an anthology at a flea market and liked those a lot. I remember not having the money for the anthology so I bought a little paperback by him instead, *How are Verses Made?* It had some poems in it, which is why I bought it, but mostly it was this HOW-TO through a political structure, which was interesting but also annoyed me at times. What stuck with me the most was the line, "Poetry is at its very root tendentious." I remember this because I had to look up *tendentious*, a word not part of the vernacular where I grew up. When I found the word in the dictionary I thought, "Really? Because a lot of poetry is boring and seems to stand for NOTHING!" At the time I knew I LOVED poetry, but liked none of the poetry we were made to read at public school. Well that's not true as I loved Dickinson a great deal, and still do. Today however I fully embrace this perception of Mayakovsky's, but I had to find it out on my own. Resisting what is said by others has always been my strategy, so as not to build my life around THEIR ideas. But today I also understand the statement differently, as poetry being something you are willing to stake your life against. Like Breton was saying we must FEEL IT! Because when you do you have arrived inside it, and can truly know it.

Emily Dickinson is a poet I have always been able to feel. She's immediate in that way. The first (Soma)tic in this book is Her. I wanted to invoke the high priestess, and She is the high priestess. Besides the fact that She's completely misunderstood as this wilting lily hiding in Her home—*what nonsense!*—She had the courage and brilliance to take centuries of poetry and make it Her very own. This exercise came out of an argument I had had with a man I knew years ago who talked about visiting the Dickinson house. He said, "No one's alive now who knew Dickinson." And I said, "That's not TRUE, there are those ENORMOUS trees in the backyard!" He said, "You know I mean PEOPLE!" And I said, "You know I ALSO mean PEOPLE!" Because I DO mean living, conscious beings, which trees ARE. Anyone who grew up in a rural setting and spent time with trees knows they're giant sentient beings who are aware of their world. Everyone wants to visit the Dickinson house, lots and lots of boards of dead wood and they clack around imagining Emily peering out windows and writing Her verse. I didn't even go inside the house for the visit to gather dirt for this first exercise in the book, just out back with the trees. That dirt around their roots is part of their very own symbiogenesis, the bacteria and other living part of the loam and the tree are one, needing one another. And the trees are very large, very old, and were alive when Dickinson was alive, and you know She touched them, leaned on them, was part of their lives and they were part of Her life. We take trees, grind them up, take that pulp, press it, make paper to write out our thoughts. Or our grocery lists, suicide notes, and marriage licenses, all the while with unmitigated hubris thinking that OUR thoughts are the thoughts to carve into the tree's body, as though they never had their own feelings and ideas. The intelligence of trees was an axiom in many ancient human cultures, but today metal and plastic rule the center of gravity. I gathered some dirt from under the trees to take home and smear on my body for the "ANOINT THYSELF" (Soma)tic. And I also peed back there in order to give back what I took, as our urine contains rich nitrogen. My friend Susie Timmons (a BRILLIANT poet everyone should read!) teased me about this as we drove away! That was a very fun visit to Emily's house!

Eileen Myles was the first living poet I ever read who embodied this idea that you are going to feel it. Myles gives us Breton's and Mayakovsky's statements and MUCH MORE! She is going to make you feel it, smell it. Her body, your body, bodies are always in her work, and trees, trees in so many poems. She's queer, and that has a lot to do with it, something I understand completely. Centuries of monotheistic domination over our bodies, telling EVERYONE that our bodies are dirty, ugly, they crave, are FOUL, these FOUL bodies ACTUALLY WANTING and thinking we deserve PLEASURE! Yeah, yeah we do! FUCK the Return To Modesty Campaign! This world is beautiful if we listen to the body's intelligence! Eileen Myles is total permission! If her work doesn't inspire readers then I can't even imagine what to do for them. Her poems are some of the most astute inquiries about separation of mind, body, and spirit. The spaces between her words and lines grapple with this. Her poems invigorate a consciousness of flesh in a world where flesh is either denying its needs or trying to make space for those needs.

I begin this book with the quote "the living and the dead give in and wave to me" from the great Robert Desnos, a poet who was destroyed by the Nazis in the death camps. You FEEL Desnos's body and soul in his writing, it's impossible not to! But who are "the living and the dead," I ask. On first reading he seems to be referring to these other people he knows, has known. But the "give in" part, well, I feel very strongly that "the living and the dead" are living and dead parts of himself. He's referring to his own awakening of his physical and spiritual bodies, and it's a SUDDEN recognition. This line is an admission of self-actualization, a rare moment of TOTAL awareness! It is in fact an encapsulated moment of Desnos genius! It's a portal to walk through, which is a perfect way to open this book of (Soma)tics.

Poetry is a blueprint of who we are at the time of writing it. Even those poets who deny the personal I, they are in there. You can't NOT be your poem, whether you are writing confessional, in strict form, or writing a conceptual poem. Steve Zultanski's amazing book *PAD* for instance, where he lifts everything in his apartment with his cock, or dick, penis, you know. It's Steve Zultanski, that poem, that movement, his catalogue of thoughts, that arrangement, HE is in there, HE is that. He is very much in there, I mean it's a poem where a man's cock is literally part of the decision-making process for the creation of the poem. What a fantastic book!

Sherwood Anderson's collection of stories *WINESBURG, OHIO* is one of those books I had read out there along the highway as a kid while selling flowers. It begins with a remarkable introductory statement called "The Book of the Grotesque," and it's about how we physically manifest trauma. Magdalena Zurawski's *THE BRUISE* is one of the rare books that transfer the anxieties of Franz Kafka for me. Kafka is a big influence on my life as a poet of (Soma)tics, his characters physically exhibiting their trauma, whether waking up as an insect, starving, or having their crimes written into their flesh. Kafka was always grappling with the abrupt intersections of the Soma and the Somatic, caving-in under it in fact!

I'm not caving-in though. I want to love this world, despite the cesspool it is rapidly becoming all around us. Because I'm queer I KNEW that in order to survive I had to love who I am. Where I grew up you would actually have to kill yourself for anyone to feel empathy for your "condition" of being queer. I've said it before, but THAT absolute need to make peace with myself has made poetry so much easier. Centuries of walls came down for me, and I'm really quite fortunate for that, but it's not a lot of fun getting there when you're emotionally and physically tormented along the way. Faggot became my name at school. And jocks would pass me in the hall and scream "IT'S AN EXIT NOT AN ENTRANCE FAG-GOT!" The definition of vile. But surviving them is sublime.

Courage is essential, and in my opinion one of the most courageous poets to ever write was Mina Loy. I LOVE her poems! She makes being human bearable when it seems nearly unendurable. In a 1917 interview she said something we should all listen closely to, words to recalibrate any fear by:

If you are very frank with yourself and don't mind how ridiculous anything that comes to you may seem, you will have a chance of capturing the symbol of your direct reaction. The antique way to live and express life was to say it according to the rules. But the modern flings herself at life and lets herself feel what she does feel, then upon the very tick of the second she snatches the images of life that fly through the brain.

For most of my life I have been studying people while working stupid jobs. And my family working in coffin factories, can, pie, detergent, cough drop, dental floss, cardboard box, ketchup, and other factories. I can still SEE my father standing on the loading dock of the coffin factory lecturing me about THE SECURITY OF HAVING A GOOD JOB while coffins are being loaded onto a truck behind him. I stood there asking myself, "Does he just REFUSE to recognize the irony of this?" I have watched immensely creative, intelligent people be reduced to their most basic instinctual drive for jobs. For years my family told me ART is a luxury. Is it though? Even in failing economies? I've watched aunts and uncles work double shifts at the factory, come home, get some beer, and watch television all night, AND THEN die young.

Something Jack Spicer wrote was, "I only know that I love strength in my friends / And greatness"—it's from "A Poem Without a Single Bird in It." No one inspires me more, and spurs me into writing more, than my peers. We're living in one of the most exciting times for poetry. Boundaries and borders of every kind are being crossed, and often crisscrossed. Having serious and lasting friendships with other poets whose work I admire has granted me unlimited access into the Soma of the poems I choose to write.

Frank Sherlock investigates the flesh in all aspects. Here's a poet who nearly died several years ago from meningitis but struggled back from the brink, and came to us a shaman poet. Frank's book *OVER HERE* has poems that are witness to the flesh rescued from the edge of transmuting beyond his control, and this is harrowing, scary, and triumphant. I had the good fortune of writing a book with Frank titled *THE CITY REAL AND IMAGINED*. These were very physical poems, meaning we set out to investigate the city together, on foot, to deeply scrutinize the details. We mixed his influence of Situationist philosophies with my leaning toward Thoreau's essay on and praxis of Walking in the best sense of Walking, or sauntering (to continue the Thoreau derivation), as though all ground is Holy. I'm very proud of what we did together through poetry. I find it rare for two poets to TRULY collaborate. If one poet is too aggressive and narcissistic, and the other defers for whatever reason, it shows in the lines. But if two poets come to work together and are interested only in each making this a pact for equal input and participation, then the strength of the lines will show this.

Bernadette Mayer is another big influence, and she has been waking people up since before I was born. Her lists of exercises to locate poetry continue to be used in classrooms all over the world. But of course United States public school poetry classes are boring because our government doesn't want poor kids excited about poetry since revolution is what they try to avoid. Poetry and the other arts must return to a place of being useful. Recently I was part of a symposium honoring Bernadette Mayer and one of the presenters said, and I quote, "There is too much writing in the world!" I challenged that position as elitist, and furthermore there is TOO MUCH WAR in the world, but never too much poetry! The world needs everyone understanding our creative viscera NOW, not later but NOW! There are nearly seven billion people on the planet at the time we're having this conversation Thom, but soon there will be nine billion. We NEED to find the way to permission, to unlock the imagination. Real change requires real thinking. The definition of art is always annoying to me. It needs LESS definition, borders that are not brick but something more porous, like pudding, yes, I prefer art with pudding borders, and you have a delicious snack as you eat your way out of it.

I have been reading and thinking about the history of the avant-garde, and what claims for art and literature different writers and artists have made within that tradition. There is an avant-garde lineage that privileges art as an autonomous space, one that doesn't have to account for its sociality, or for a particular political or economic position. I consider most of

the art that we're both interested in to be very against this idea of autonomy. But I have also noticed another division with a tentative post–avant-garde that would like to sequester "activism" from what George Oppen called the "action" of writing and art. Through your work and the work of those you mention above, you seem to be saying that art/writing can have a direct effect on health, well-being, and the body of the person inasmuch as that body extends and defines a body politic—a realm where the social and the political are both produced. In fact, you are insisting that health, well-being, and the body politic *depend* on art/poetry. So one thing I'm wondering is if you'd care to further define the relationship between politics and art. I love that the (S)E are trying to be *useful*, to do something. And that poetry, for you, has the capacity to effect change, whereas I think most people would dismiss it as a "luxury," or simply as useless, excessive, besides the point of any "real" social movement.

First of all I find the term *post-avant* offensive. And I go further and say that ANY group calling themselves avant-garde WAS and IS political. Otherwise they were merely experimental. As Kaia Sand and Michael Hennessey have said, both in their own ways, but very similarly, avant-garde denotes the community of the body politic, in fact IS the action where there is room for much to do together. The term *post-avant* was invented by and for lazy scabs who want to bust the unions of art community. Post-avant is a term for the slums of the elite where NO ONE has to be endured as a living, breathing, viable resource. The post-avant is a crime against the possibilities of this world. The post-avants fail themselves and fail the rest of us just by their nature of saying THERE IS NO ROOM for holding to the creative axis. The post-avant is for hacks who need an excuse for being hacks. I'm NOT LIVING in someone's POST-ANYTHING by the fucking way! We are not the leftovers! The belief is wrong that we are! What IS ACTUALLY at hand is a richer, more complex world we find ourselves in, so fuck this term and those who believe in it!

And by the way my friend I'm tired of being asked to define WHY ART is useful! How about someone explaining WHY WAR is useful? How about THAT! Tell me why war is useful and THEN I'll give you reasons for art! If it were not for art you and I would be DEAD from the misery we could never rid ourselves of without it, HOW IS THAT for an answer? ANYONE who has loved this world with art knows what I say to be true!

To switch gears just a little, I am also wondering, on a practical level, if you could maybe go into some depth about your process with regard to any of the exercises? Could you describe in detail the way a particular exercise came about, maybe one that was very difficult for you to arrive at? Or, if you prefer, perhaps you could describe a few of them, just to give some sense of how you arrived at them. I know you take extensive notes in your preparation to create an exercise. What else goes into the process? How much adjusting goes into the process after an exercise has been undertaken—after you have "tested" it yourself? How much "fine-tuning" do the exercises take before you can "write them up"? When are they "finished"?

Through (Soma)tic practice all studies of language, science, religion, and different artistic disciplines have a potential place in the poem's creation. The daily organic functions of Soma and Somatic hold secrets to poetry in plain view. The poet's task to engage the breathing, living world becomes more urgent when enacted in tandem with a human world that is increasingly more technologically efficient, dependent, and dangerous.

Everything about them continues to surprise me, including the poems. It's inexplicable how THE POEMS come. I have resisted more than once the way a particular poem wants to take shape from these experiences with the exercises, but then, finally, if I surrender, it gives itself a life. It's painful to shut up a part of you to let another have full reign. But it's my goal in many ways, to trust that what led me here knows what's best. And the best things in life we're led to are led by the heart. The brain wants to take charge when we arrive, but resisting that hostile takeover can only increase the pleasure of the day when we SEE what is possible!

About DOING the exercises, though. I've been asked about the note taking during the exercise, like HOW do those notes translate into poems? Fair enough question, right? The notes are our being our own stenographers for a time, taking the actual directives of the movements, and at times too being asked to write completely without present thought, but with present sensation. In shaping the poems there are often lines that jump out and present themselves as lines for the poem, yes, but very often lines present ways to entire new structures that were not even considered at the time of doing the exercise. Trusting the notes. Trusting too that at the time of carrying the notes around to form the poem is its own kind of exercise, BEING in the world with the notes. Does that make sense?

The exercises are designed to fling us OUT OF our routines. Routine is what puts a cap on the imagination. And we all have routines. And most of the routines we have can get out of hand, and we can find ourselves most uncomfortable living outside of them. Especially if you have children, or need to be ever so responsible. The more responsibility, the more routine, it's a given. So the exercises give EVERYONE—no matter who—the frame to bust out of the routine, if only for a little while. The exercises get us to deliberately engage the world in unexpected ways. It's vital to jostle loose the amazing things each of us has hiding inside. I defy anyone to prove we're not all creative beings!

And it's true too that many things are at work simultaneously. There has already been an enormous body of research to refer to, and that research can help us form and demonstrate other ideas for reading the world. For instance, piezoelectricity led me to my development of a dream therapy, or rather a means by which to recall dreams upon waking, a storage space for remembering. And IT WORKS! Through the use of crystal-infused water it works! My hatred of sleep put dreaming to work. While the pope worries about my "wasted" faggot sperm, I worry about my wasted dreaming, so I want to remember and use those valuable dreams. My dream therapy is a kind of condom for the imagination, hmm, or something. The metaphor is wrong, but anyway. The unexpected side effect has been involuntary astral projections, out-of-body experiences. That's a whole other story, and an entirely different kind of poem I'm writing from those experiences, but at the same time they are (Soma)tic poems.

Another example is Ernst Chladni discovering the actual form of sound. He put sand on a metal plate then ran a bow along the edge of the plate and the sand jumped into the shape of an hourglass, or rather a guitar or violin. It's amazing that he discovered that! In the end it's no surprise that the shape of sound is the body of a violin, or guitar, any more than it is a surprise that Soma (the divine) lives inside Somatic (the body). What IS surprising is that nowhere do I find the question, "HOW did human beings KNOW the shape of sound, before Chladni, to make these instruments the shape they made them?" How marvelous! Experimenting with sound has been an essential part of the (Soma)tic experience. (Soma)tics is a praxis that is totally experiential. An experiment is an engagement, right? It is the will of the questioner set into motion.

In my continued research of the possibilities of (Soma)tics, sound has come forward as a sense to be experienced beyond the auditory. Studies on water's absorption of sound have impacted my process concerns. The average human adult has 50 trillion cells, which are roughly 75 percent water. If a lake or puddle is going to be disturbed or displaced by sound, then it follows that human flesh would also. During my first endeavors with (Soma)tic poetry I wrote a series of seven poems. Each one was written after eating a single color of food for a day. For the blue poem I listened to Bobby Vinton's "Blue Velvet" on a continuous loop from 6 a.m. until midnight. Further research led me to the information that sounds that are not language gravitate to one part of the human brain. But as soon as words are heard, those sounds go to an entirely different part of the brain to be decoded. The "Blue Velvet" experiment felt oppressive as a result, my mind constantly decoding, constantly hearing words instead of creating words. I later listened to Donald Byrd's song "Cristo Redentor" on a continuous loop for 108 hours nonstop, or four and a half days. The song is an instrumental, and the experience was a chilling set of beautiful waves, an ocean to ride and write on.

Everyone has been made into who they are, for better or worse. But it's in that making where our unique lenses are forged. (Soma)tics is a chance—or a series of chances—to deliberately experience our own lens, to see how and why we see what we see. The resulting poems are the fruits of the lens brought into sharpest focus. Lorine Niedecker says in one of her amazing letters to a friend, "Early in life I looked back of our buildings to the lake and said, 'I am what I am because of all this—I am what is around me—those woods have made me . . .'" YES! YES! YESYESYES!

Niedecker was KNOWING she was the world. There was an experience I had at a very young age watching a deer decay over a period of time, and this STUDY—I did make a study of it—gave me no pleasure other than the fact that we're solidly HERE, always; kill yourself and your reproachable cells will face the miscibility of this world regardless of need. The true needs are the pulsing soil and hammering clouds around us, the needs we ignore. (Soma)tics is one possible reconciliatory motion. Don't kill yourself! Write a poem and FIND yourself! Poems of use, here; let us defy the cranky and abysmal declaring an end to what is possible. Saying that there is nothing new to try is said by the truly stupid and lazy. You couldn't possibly TRY EVERYTHING in one lifetime so SHUT UP and SHUT OFF that fucking television, and could we PLEASE get to work LIVING IN THIS WORLD? Poetry is living! Let's live!

Okay, okay, let me answer you more directly. So the (Soma)tics I create are clearly from my own filter as a human being who happened to form the way in which I did. The way in which I DO, I should keep this present tense, since I'm alive, right? My hope is that people do the (Soma)tics enough for them to see where they can form their own. Does that make sense? I feel very fortunate to be AWAKE in this world. It's so easy to SLEEP here! It's a sleepy business, often, due to the stresses imposed on us. Life WILL get harder, and soon, as the human population grows AND GROWS and the wars THE WARS! One of the more recent (Soma)tics was the one where I litter. I just know it's going to be figured out THAT I'M THE ONE who has been littering in wealthy neighborhoods with messages written into my litter. But WHY DO THIS? Because this world is beautiful, and I'm here, knowing it's beautiful, and I'm tired of some people having money to BREATHE while others suffer. Suffering is a big part of what I look to for guidance. Suffering and love. Resistance is most urgent. Resistance is the real magic. As soon as you set yourself down the path of NOT being agreeable to the directives of others your poetry becomes THAT LIFE! It becomes YOUR POEMS, YOUR LIFE!

And anyone can look at the (Soma)tic poetry exercises for any other discipline and make them work. For instance the dancer and choreographer Ellie Goudie-Averill of Stone Depot Dance Lab has been dancing to the (Soma)tics. I was at a restaurant in Philadelphia with Joshua Beckman and she stopped to say hello. When I told her that Joshua was working with me to publish a collection of (Soma)tics she explained that wherever an exercise says WRITE she replaces it with DANCE. "It's that easy," she said. I love watching what is possible, and Ellie is one of those brilliant AWAKE artists who know so much is possible. There's also a filmmaker named Courtney Shumway, she's using film to create through (Soma)tics. I truly believe EVERYTHING is a form of collaboration.

Recently I was in Asheville, North Carolina, to visit my old friend Elizabeth Kirwin. We exchanged healing bodywork. I gave her deep-tissue massage with hot towels, something I was trained to do many years ago. She gave me craniosacral therapy. On the seventh night I had a dream that I was in a small blue room with an old Japanese woman. She patted my hand and said, "You waited too long to see me, now you must wait until the next life." She went through a door, closing it behind her. When I tried to open the door it became part of the wall and disappeared, and I realized there was no longer a way to get to her.

When I woke I knew exactly who this woman was. In 1989 my friend Sylvia wanted to take me to Japan to celebrate my one-year anniversary of being macrobiotic. We had met a couple of years before when she had a cocaine addiction and my boyfriend at the time was her drug dealer. It's funny how things come together. But Sylvia was a millionaire, and tried to convince me that money was nothing, and that it was blood money from her family and that we should use it for good. We were both macrobiotic then and she wanted us to go see the traditional methods of making miso, and where the kukicha and bancha twigs were dried for tea. We were also going to go to Kyoto to visit the poet Cid Corman, who I was corresponding with at the time. She enthusiastically encouraged me to travel with her, and to not worry about the money.

In the end I said no. Growing up poor left me with a sense of unworthiness that I've since dealt with, but at the time my guilt of taking a gift that lavish was more than I could manage. So Sylvia went without me, and sent me postcards, and brought back some delicious teas and other things, including a beautiful handmade suribachi bowl for making fresh gamazio. But a week into her trip without me I had a dream that a Japanese woman—maybe in her early sixties—came to me and said, "You made a mistake, you were supposed to meet me. We did everything we could to get you here but you are stubborn. There is still time to see me. I have something important to tell you." This dream haunted me for years, as much as the new dream will most likely haunt me. I know that it was the same woman, twenty-two years later. And since there is nothing more that I can do to meet her in this lifetime I have dedicated a (Soma)tic poetry exercise in honor of the mysterious woman I failed to meet.

Although you have touched on it somewhat here, will you speak about your experience teaching workshops with the exercises? How it has pushed you to explore pedagogical problems, problems of how one fosters learning? I would be curious to hear what you have observed in workshop participants, as well as what kind of feedback you have received. I love too what you say about wanting to avoid mentorship, identifying strongly with this antiauthoritarian (I almost wrote "anti-Arthurian") position myself. Let's say you were given a grant to start a school: What would happen at this school? How would it be organized and function? How, also, might it function pedagogically through the (Soma)tic Exercises?

I only ever attended one poetry workshop in my life, it was when I was nineteen, and it was with the poet William Stafford and I truly disliked him! It disgusted me hearing him TELL

US what our poems REALLY MEANT through subtext! He was WRONG, and siphoned ALL of our oxygen! My hatred of authority has saved my poetry more than once.

When people come to my workshops the first time, they're confused that we're not sitting in folding chairs tinkering with the guts of old European meter. We're hands-on the world, and do so together. I'm not THE TEACHER, I'm merely a guide and look to the participants as much as they look to me—I'm a participant too, in other words. If they are students then so am I—that's how these workshops run. I do NOT believe in mentorship; in fact I have friends I love dearly who mention their "protégés" and I vomit a little in my mouth upon hearing this, OY how I do! Mentors should be destroyed, that's my advice to anyone with a mentor! Destroy them before they destroy you! The more you RESIST the more you learn! It's in developing that muscle of resistance where we learn to listen deeply and with great care to our own thoughts and actions. This is where the best we have awaits us!

When I conduct a workshop we reach for the WHY of poetry. There are plenty of places people can go if they want to learn the HOW. When HOW comes up for us it's HOW the world works in order to get to the WHY of poetry. There are too many times in our lives where we have things defined for us and that's it, it's just accepted that these drips of water coming out of the sky is rain. (Soma)tics is picking up where we left off with these questions about rain when we were kids. The vitality of water hammers every aspect of our lives, so it's not such an easy answer, and that's what we want to discover in order to write with purpose. The science of appreciation is an actual science where much can be learned, and it's learned through going into the world, no matter how stupid, no matter how crazy, no matter how awkward. In fact the more our awkwardness is tested the better our poems become, and this is always true, always true!

NOTES FROM 4 (SOMA)TIC
POETRY WORKSHOPS

*The words are only part of the poetic
formula: the rest is ritual, and the
reason in* them *must contend with the
mechanics of magic-making in* it—*and
must not win.*

—LAURA RIDING

The following are examples of (Soma)tic workshops I designed and conducted: two in New York City, one in Seattle, and one in Philadelphia. They are for everyone and anyone no matter how much one knows about poetry. Each of us has the potential to create if we are willing to strike out. I never want to be anything but a student of this world who travels with other students, anxious, disturbed, always eager to imagine yet another kind of handle on the door.

(Soma)tic Poetry at St. Mark's Poetry Project, NYC

VANISHING CONCERNS: We will take time to discuss VANISHING and what it means to each of us. We will discuss the pressures of being physical in a world where the physical breaks down its particles, vanishing from form to form to return and return in different manifestations.

VANISHING REFLUX: This exercise is loosely based on a 500-year-old Rosicrucian magical practice that involves keen concentration and honest evaluation of personal retention of images. With the original magical practice to shift and/or persuade the physical/mental of a given space we would stand at its threshold, fully view it, then close our eyes to imagine what was seen. When we open our eyes we look for WHAT WE MISSED. The process is repeated with each visit to the space, each time building its entire structure in the brain until, finally, it has been fully captured in the mind. We would then be able to meditate on that space whenever needed. For instance we could calm an agitated person in our meditation, having the room plugged into our conscious mind. What we are taking from this practice is to see what we miss and build ideas on why we miss what we miss to generate language for our poems.

VANISHING REFLUX EXERCISE: The weather report PROMISES a beautiful day for Saturday, October 11. After talking about VANISHING CONCERNS together we will go into the adjoining church garden. We will spend a few minutes finding a spot to sit, on a bench or on the ground. Spend a few more minutes taking in the sounds, smells, and of course images. Keep notepad and pen nearby. Close your eyes and relax for a minute. Then OPEN your eyes suddenly and without blinking use your eyes as you would a camera lens to drink in everything you see. Then close your eyes. With your eyes closed IMAGINE what you have just seen as best as you can, making notes to yourself, naming things as you see them, putting them in your mind's storage. Open your eyes again and look closely. Very carefully note what you had forgotten was in the picture before you closed your eyes. Take notes about this thing and where it is and how it fits into the picture from where you are sitting. Repeat this process several times, each time noticing something else you had missed when closing your eyes. Once you have a few items that were missed, walk over to them. What are these things you let vanish? What do they mean to you? Take notes, take as many notes as you can, NOTES are where our poems are waiting for us. Look again at one of the objects, imagine it different colors, frozen, melting, imagine it vanishing, imagine it vanishing with or without your help. How is it something that is ignored, something easily ignored by you and others? When do you feel ignored? Touch an elbow, randomly touch your cheek, be completely free to be DIFFERENT at this moment. Then take your notepad and write QUICKLY and without thinking, write quickly, write quickly, keep writing, write as much as you can at this point.

(Soma)tic Poetry at St. Mark's Poetry Project, NYC

BETWEEN THE GENDERS: We will discuss gender. Did you ever ask your mother or father what your name would have been if you had been born the opposite sex? We will ask ourselves how many genders there are, and how many are possible in a world that very much wants a simple answer of two.

ROSEMARY BETWEEN THE GENDERS: Rosemary is a foundational herb used in many different magic spells. Rosemary spikes the groundwork for infusing a new set of rules to be implemented and managed, whether for transforming the physical or abstract dimensions. We will each have a sprig of rosemary to carry with us for this exercise. We are free to go wherever we want inside the building or out in the yard, or walk down the street if we want. Before sniffing the rosemary take some notes about your gender, or write about your feelings and ideas about gender in general. Take those initial notes to break open space in yourself for gender. Then take a few deep breaths of fresh air, then squeeze the leaves of the rosemary to release the oils and take a nice DEEP BREATH. Now, imagine yourself a different gender. What do you feel like when you imagine this? What are your hands like? Your feet? How are you walking as this Other? What name would you like to have as this Other? Take another DEEP breath of your rosemary and say that name out loud to yourself. Really get INSIDE this Other you. It might even be good to go up to the restroom and look into the mirror and SAY your Other name. Close your eyes, then open them and say your Other name into the mirror. HOW DOES THE WORLD RECEIVE YOU AS THE OTHER GENDER? How different will the world treat you as this Other? Take notes, take as many notes as you can manage, pause and take another sniff of rosemary

183

whenever you need. If you decide to walk down the street go into a store and look at things you buy on a regular basis. Then look at things you might buy if you were another gender. Take some time looking at these items and imagine buying them, owning them, being with them. Take more D E E P breaths of rosemary whenever you want, and take lots of notes. Try writing notes slowly, as slow as you can manage, then write Q U I C K L Y and without think-ing.

SPLAB, SEATTLE

(SOMA)TIC POETRY WORKSHOP

RESILIENT TRIANGLE: We will each meditate on the room, and choose one person to study. Then find two stationary objects off the ground: a window, clock, light fixture, etc. Now with your mind draw a connecting line between the person you have studied and the other two objects. Take notes about the contents of your triangle, what exactly is INSIDE this triangle you have created. Then imagine the triangle in different forms of light, temperature, different seasons, even imagine the objects within the triangle different colors. Imagine someone you love inside the triangle, floating. Imagine them sick. Then dying. Imagine yourself inside the triangle aging, dying. Imagine random objects flying into the triangle, like a carton of milk thrown through it. Imagine a dozen cartons of milk hovering inside the triangle, then slowly pouring milk to the ground. These notes will in some way become notes of our courage to be in this world.

HUMAN HIBERNACULUM: The hibernaculum is where an animal goes to be safe during periods of hibernation. We will create the human hibernaculum with our bodies as a place of highly charged energy. We will break into groups of five. One person will sit in the middle to take notes, while the others stand in a circle around them. We will stand with our backs to the center and with our right hands we will find the carotid artery in the neck of the person to our left until everyone is feeling a pulse and having their pulse taken. We will HUM a deep, low hum from time to time to connect with each other. This rope of blood pulsing in a circle above the person seated taking their notes will shift every five minutes as we keep changing who is sitting in the center to take notes. Everyone will get the opportunity to sit in the hibernaculum to take five minutes of writing.

"CRISTO REDENTOR": The hibernaculum will have been physically challenging, and even stressful on us all. For this part of the workshop we will sit quietly and listen to Donald Byrd's "CRISTO REDENTOR" at top volume. This jazz song is the only song I know of where a gospel choir is used from start to finish, yet they sing no words. The song is 5 minutes 42 seconds long. For the first minute 52 seconds Byrd's trumpet isn't heard at all. By the time he enters we are SWEPT through the chords with a force that is difficult to prepare for. After listening to the song in silence we will listen to it again, but this time write nonstop for the duration of the song. Sound engages our brains differently whether sounds are language or not. As soon as language is heard we begin to decode; different hemispheres of the brain handle these different concerns. With "CRISTO REDENTOR" we have the rare opportunity of hearing the human voice for a sustained amount of time without needing to decode language; the voices are themselves instruments of the pleasure and joy of song. The redemptive quality of song. Byrd asks that we make the Redeemer our very own, in our own way.

PHILADELPHIA

(SOMA)TIC POETRY WORKSHOP

CREATION SONG: As we know, humans have created the existence of the world over and over in magnificent stories. This workshop is being conducted in the home of poet Eleanor Wilner while I house-sit. The room with the piano has many sculptures, paintings, heirlooms, dolls, giant hand-carved mirrors, and various other beautiful things from around the world. While I play the piano in and out of chord/discord, roam the room and fabricate a creation song of your own for us. Reinvent the things you see; for instance, the little Buddha statue might instead be an ancient astronaut who came to Earth to impregnate primitive humans and alter our DNA. There will be a stool close to the piano for anyone who wishes to sit with an ear pressed to the piano while taking notes.

REIKI SONG: Form a line bending around the corner of a doorway into another room, ending out of sight and earshot of the head of the line. We will have our right hand on the top of the head of the person in front of us, the person at the front of the line is seated, taking notes. The 2 or 3 people at the very back of the line HUM A STEADY, DEEP HUM, sending this electrical pulse through the line. We will switch every 5 minutes until everyone has been at every stage of the line, humming, writing, sending and receiving the electrical current. In the end we will gather in a circle, hold hands and HUM TOGETHER VERY DEEPLY, AS LOUD AS WE CAN. We will write again for another 10 minutes without pause.

PASSIVE PARTY OUTFIT SONG: I will sit at a table with various wigs, nail polish, lipstick and other makeup, hairpins, hats, scarves, necklaces, brooches, sunglasses, and various colored shirts. A very small painting of a party in a village will be on the table. All of you will sit on the other side of the room and instruct me to put on the items. There will be a pair of binoculars to better see the painting on the table, and anything else you wish to see. You must also decide if you are getting me ready for the party in the painting, or getting me ready to crash the party in the painting, or getting me ready to THROW the party in the painting. Yell out requests for cocktails and food, yell out requests for songs to be played, insist on a live band or a DJ.

15 (SOMA)TIC READING ENHANCEMENTS

(Soma)tic Reading Enhancements are an extension of my (Soma)tic Poetics, in fact they're actually not just an extension but are the poetics themselves, as the same praxis applies, for the origin of writing is locked with the origin of reading. As the writing of (Soma)tics is an engagement with the thing of things and the spirit of things, so are the (Soma)tic Reading Enhancements.

The enhancements for each book were chosen intuitively, rather than randomly, a structure derived from initial sensations upon receiving a particular book. It is my wish as a poet to encourage readers to not be passive and to take credit for a poem's absorption. After all, we each bring a unique set of experiences and circumstances to filter and digest poems, making them part of ourselves in our own way. Try these (Soma)tic Reading Enhancements, and maybe you will want to alter the enhancement as you read, or create a different one. Let's encourage one another to have full participatory poetry reading!

To the muscle that bends language,

CAConrad

Boil 4 tablespoons of whole cloves in a quart of water. Boil on high flame for 5 minutes. Shut flame off and let the infusion cool to a hot/warm drinkable temperature. Now, VIGOROUSLY brush your teeth and gums for a full 5 minutes. Brush, brush, brush hard, brush, YEAH, REALLY BRUSH tooth by tooth and GUMS, especially give the gums an intense, hard brushing. Now, sit down and take a mouthful of the clove infusion, but don't swallow, just let it soak into the freshly brushed teeth and gums. Then SPIT IT INTO an empty pan or bucket. Start reading, feeling the clove treatment TINGLE and soothe, and move your lips deliberately, and tongue, whisper the poems, speak them, whisper. Take another mouthful of your clove infusion, AND THIS TIME VIGOROUSLY swish it in your mouth, between your teeth, and from cheek to cheek, really swish it around, then SPIT IT INTO your bucket. Whisper the next poem, then read it again with a louder voice. Stop midway, maybe at page 55, the poem ending "hemorrhage / of / air / into everyone's / sky," and make some more clove infusion, but this time for a nice footbath. Scrub your feet VIGOROUSLY before dipping them into the hot clove infusion. Ah, now continue. Occasionally flip to the cover and say aloud "BETTY'S REVENGE!" which is the name of the painting on the cover! Are you FILLING with the sensations of poetry and clove infusion? "a threat designated me at birth / attuned to close-calls / and violent eruptions of selfhoods / built on faults / to treat with a homeopathic / sibilant whisper / sssss / achieve / a hatred sealant"

NATHANIEL SIEGEL'S *TONY* (YO YO LABS PRESS)

You need a can of whipped cream, as we're working with the lower chakras. Put a plastic garbage bag under a chair and get naked. Don't be shy, I'm not asking you to do this onstage, you're alone, you're safe, IT'S GREAT! Shake your whipped cream and squirt a good lather of it on the seat of your chair, and the back of the chair. Sit down gently, gently into the whipped-cream seat. Did you ever sit on a lather of whipped cream before to read poetry? If not, an entire new file of memory will be created in your brain. Every once in a while spray a little more whipped cream here and there, and move your limbs and back into it; READ ALOUD while doing so, and READ LOUD AS YOU CAN as a matter of fact. Midway through the book, somewhere near the stanza ending "manager driving me home / putting music on / not getting he's trying to tell me something," stand and feel the whipped cream like a luxurious and strange garment. If you're adventurous, as I hope you are, try gently sticking the whipped cream nozzle into your asshole and inject the creamy dairy product up there. Go ahead—remember, no one's looking. NOW sit back down. How is that? It's really good, isn't it? Admit it, it's good, right? Whipped-cream enema, something everyone would love if they gave it a shot. You'll never forget this marvelous book: "be caught off guard in a pool hall a naked guy / hold my friend all night until she goes for her AIDS test / hold my friends hand 48 hours in a coma no sleep / a vision of her the sand: light lifting up a reflection a lake"

FRANK SHERLOCK'S *OVER HERE* (FACTORY SCHOOL PRESS)

Is there a shopping mall near you? I went to one in Philadelphia, The Gallery, for this book. Shopping malls are filled with the strangest opportunities to engage poems anew. The elevator in this mall was clear glass, and I got on, stood facing the mall below, and read. People would get on, and it would move up, then down, then be still for a little while as I read, "It is difficult to / provide anything / more than skeleton / for the peace / though this skin / is seeded w/ nerve / endings flinching / at the prospect / of touch." Have you ever hidden in the middle of a round rack of pants? The busy department store was perfect for hiding, reading, smelling the fresh cotton and polyester, possibly made by very tired hands: "The genocide / comics / are lullabies / a rest / from hearts / from fatigues." In the furniture department there are very comfortable chairs to read in: "The void is here the invisible distance that makes this aesthetic boom / Shatters dispersal of selves figure into a common finger tongue brain." Near the pet food you can always find poisons and traps for other animals, unwanted animals. Have prepared on a roll of tape such messages as STOP THE KILLING AND PET YOUR CAT, and such, then sit on a sparkling new bicycle for sale, and read, "I am a passenger sitting in a suspicious / way w/ a yearn for the new to be older / Strangers become friends even if they are sometimes objects / The white star is on the blue field / There is a black eagle on a red sea / Crates have brought w/ them the dead people & the letters / sent from loved ones when the dead people were alive." Buy some bubble gum and ride the escalator up, up, up, and down, and back around, reading, "So it is decided that / men who pose for pictures w/ guns have terrible taste / in eyewear Some faces reflect the light of others Every lake / tastes different & even at the end the land / remains a place to fall in love."

KATHRYN L. PRINGLE'S *RIGHT NEW BIOLOGY*
(FACTORY SCHOOL PRESS)

Do this on a hot, humid day, as I did; it's an especially sublime experience on such a day. Wrap your naked body in maps, atlas pages, or even imaginary maps you draw yourself. Scotch-tape your suit of PLACES the lines as highways, lines as borders, take us by car, plane, solely imagined. THEN put your OTHER clothes on over your DIRECTIONS TO SUIT THE WORLD. Remember to bring drinking water, because if you pass out you'll miss the best parts of the poems. Don't pass out. Where do you want to go out there with your fellow citizens? They're not noticing the bulk under your normal human clothes, don't worry about it. On your way to your public location to read, if you shoplift, or commit other crimes, and they strip-search you: MAPS! Let them find their own way. If you arrive at the location, THIS book senses location(s), note she wrote with her own body at the start: "This book could not have been written without the influence of many Presidents of the United States of America and Sigmund Freud." Are you sweating into your maps? Isn't it divine? Your sweat permeating mountain chains FEED the Mississippi FEED the sea! What is over your heart? Go to a public restroom to open your shirt if you don't remember. Reading this poet, rub that artery of highways while reading to send along what you read: "a gift is the city and the setting of work / a gift of the foreherein Organism old also / these phantasms spin / around, they drive / absurd universes." Take the directions when they come. INHALE, she writes: "INHALES / mind is two lines, or stands / a singing oracle / a swinging oracle, able sung." We're the book, we are. It's amazing.

AKILAH OLIVER'S *A TOAST IN THE HOUSE OF FRIENDS* (COFFEE HOUSE PRESS)

Maybe it was the trees on the cover, or the NEED for something MOVING around me, but I took this book out to the protected wildlife parks around Philadelphia and found a secluded stream, first for my feet, then . . . Bring a battery-powered radio, turn it to a talk-radio station, but put it far enough away that you can hear it but can't make out what is said. Faint, keep it faint, go and adjust it if you can understand them, as we want the voices to be clearly voices, but the words unattainable with our senses. Get your feet in the moving water and start reading: "language is leaving me: ahhhhh—this victimization shit / is not stable and the victors: / when are we going to safari / we: [astounded exclamation] / nancy reagan out of my head." This is a book, and it feels as if it is written right into your skin when you read it. I found an old scuba mask, and if you have one please wear it and rest your head in the stream, submerging your ears at least for the reading of one poem: "well the point is, things were calm down / here for a while and the world was little. i want to be big like you. or i / want you not vast, not dead, not gone, but human small and here. i am / so selfish. that is what i really want. to see you again. to oil your scalp. to / hear you walk in the door, say *ma i'm home*. give me a chance to say / *welcome home son*. or when leaving, *don't forget your hat*. what do you wear / out there?" That was the one I read underwater, under running water. This book needs time to be alone between poems. How is the water? How is today for you, reading Akilah's poems? "i'd like all the stone butches to wave their hands in the air right now, wave em / like they just don't care / (it seems to be unfortunate but true, corporate spell check does not recognize you / we are all too young to remember this"

MEL NICHOLS'S *CATALYTIC EXTERIORIZATION PHENOMENON* (EDGE BOOKS)

Make A LOT of ice cubes in your freezer the night before. Make an ice sling, it's very easy: use 2 plastic bags from the grocery store, fill them with ice, put these in a towel, tie the towel around your neck, but make certain that the ice is near your face at all times. Naked is best, of course. So get naked. Put your feet in a bucket of hot water and crushed garlic (4 or 5 cloves). Be ready to add more hot water and ice as you read, "I like the letters of the alphabet that slide downhill / somehow we all expected to become exasperated little gods" WHOA, this book gets you gets you gets you! WHY THE ICE YOU ASK? Why ask?, it's ice, it's poetry, it's all good, no one's getting hurt, right? Can you TASTE the garlic through your bare feet? It's nice, it's like eating through your feet while reading, right? What weird and lovely creatures we are! Rest your chin on the ice, SMELL the ice, inhale the cool air. It's summer while I'm doing this, now, and lovely, the poems make me happy, "if I'm going to have to bite heads off they / damn well better taste good / it occurs to me" I mean REALLY, can you TASTE IT, "the bad guys were there in their bad guy uniforms / our bus driver was wearing a fake bad guy uniform / so he could go inside to get us food and cigarettes / [commercial break] / back at the mansion water sprinklers / water the lawn in the pouring rain" From time to time it's good to read, then close your eyes and take a DEEP BREATH of the ice, a big ice sniff. Touch your tongue to the cubes, hold one in your bared teeth through the reading of one poem, then SPIT it back into your ice sling and read the poem aloud, have you ever felt such things while reading? It's beautiful to feel.

HOA NGUYEN'S *HECATE LOCHIA* (HOT WHISKEY PRESS)

There really are patches of grass in Philadelphia where the yuppie purebred dogs have NOT made their purebred toilets. That's where I went for this book, this patch I know of, a DE-LICIOUS patch of dirt, weeds, bugs, pebbles and bits of glass and metal, plastic-bag tumbleweeds. Wherever you are, whatever climate, whatever the earth, be in it for this book. I buried my bare feet after digging a hole with a sharp stone. It's good to have water out there. It is very hot and humid in Philadelphia in August, and I LOVE hot and humid weather, LOVE to FEEL the air, and pour the water onto my face while reading. "And I do think it's true that men stole / the magical instruments of women / & we were too busy / with ordinary life / to worry about this" If eating dirt is too much for you then smell it at least, SMELL the grass. The grass sweats chlorophyll, or I'm smelling myself in the grass, but it's kind of nice. But I ate a little of the dirt with some water, A H, gritty and weird while reading, "I might literally shut down / like a bug little legs / curled in the air" Feel O K about stopping midway to dig around, digest the poems and dirt, dig around, digest, dig into the earth and make little dirt castles for whoever is small enough to move in. There were enough beer can tabs for me to make a little table with four chairs. Remember this book with the earth covering your feet, "The 'perfect red king' / is a man becoming a woman / and bleeding every month / 'Fixed with a triple nail' / This is hard work / becoming a woman" and you will believe everything in here with the best parts of you working for it.

JENN MCCREARY'S : *AB OVO* : (DUSIE PRESS)

Bring all of this: bread, nuts, seeds, honey, water with lemon and orange slices. Take a chair someplace in your house or apartment where you N E V E R sit, someplace you would never even C O N S I D E R sitting. Like in a hallway, in a corner facing the corner, in the bathroom, or U P on a table, let's do it! This enhancement, and this book, contains a variety of different pregnancies. So sit in a place you would N E V E R sit, sit there with your plate of food, and water, make something new of the body you've known your home to be. Eat some of the food, drink some of the water, slowly, chew a long, long time. This is about being the poems of this book now, "...what the gardens can / do is import the world outside. when borders / are undefined, lines may be lost or may cease / to be. the ground beneath your feet becomes / or does not." Let's let it *become* beneath our feet. Where you are, put a plant there after you're finished reading the book. A new plant, a small, young plant. Not a lot of light? A philodendron for low light then. "the walls of this room have become the world / all around." This book, the plant, the reading, it's all going to S H I F T you, unless you're unmovable, but I bet these poems will jar you as only good poems can jar. "It's almost like the ocean. it's nothing / like the ocean. in that space / where no one else / is. it's such a long way / down. & strange. / my ears revolve for wolves. I find my footing / & walk across the air / to where you are."

195

These poems for me came from lower chakras, they're so marvelously spare they need our flanks to shake the storage of memory files loose. Take a string, not a sewing thread, something a little thicker and more durable, and something made of fiber, not plastic. Make certain the string is long enough to reach into your pants, around your crotch and ass, and out the back. You should have a good 12 inches of string hanging out the front of your pants, and the exact same amount hanging out the back of your pants. Make sure you lubricate the string that's against your skin, and be generous in lubricating it, we don't want to get rope burns from reading Joe's book, we want it beautiful instead. NO ONE is going to notice the string, so don't worry, and even if they do, they're busy, and won't let it stay in their minds for more than a minute. Go out into your town or city, or wherever you live where there are people. Test the string before leaving, pull it from the front, then pull it from the back. How is that? Is it nice? Of course it is, it's perfect for poems! Find a place to lean and read, "There are seasons here / if you squint. And there's / relief in the landscape's / sloughed off cusps of color / fallen over the familiar / landmarks, the familiar / trash—things that last." There's something beautiful about being with these quiet poems jarring our insides, while in public. Now pull your string, then reach to the other side and pull your string again, and read, "dusk dims / between leaves / on the tree / whose name / I refuse to find." I put the string RIGHT IN my ass crack, which made me totally aware of my surroundings, "Enough to make / the foliage / flinch, / wind slits. / Music sifts / out of a house." Music not just coming out of things around us, but from these poems as well, "how the light / makes do. / A thrust of / things— / a world— / words— / crush / against / the margin of you."

ERICA KAUFMAN'S *CENSORY IMPULSE* (FACTORY SCHOOL PRESS)

Go to the middle of an overpass and stare down at the traffic without blinking for as long as you can. As soon as you blink open the book. Let the traffic and road below frame the book as you read. Open yourself to FEELING urges to spout off words, lines, entire poems as loud as you want whenever you want. You're reading poetry, you have the world's permission to feel URGES and FEEL urges. Smells, sounds, even taste sensations come up with the cars. The filth of exhaust, do you get it? Stop from time to time, to close your eyes and hum a hummmmming all your own, lifting to high hummmm, low hummm, hummmmmm your hum. All of it's getting into you out here, the poems, the pulsing travel of words and cars? "this is a vocabulary of possession / this is why i won't meet you / in the road a curb under an insect / shaped fountain i bring / a trampoline to the park / offer up a bench / say my blood is somewhere / it's not important / like distance the how long / of intimate the panic / that shuts any mind down / conquer the hill feel it / please use these anecdotes / as an introduction"

ROB HALPERN'S *DISASTER SUITES* (PALM PRESS)

Does it storm where you live? If it doesn't, try sitting in the shower under an umbrella with a VERY LOUD recording of a thunderstorm playing. In Philadelphia we have the real thing, and I checked the weather reports for the PERFECT SUMMER STORM. Ah, and did I find it! Suites they are, and reading them in the middle of a torrential downpour with frightening lightning and thunder made the music OMNIPRESENT as few experiences of reading have done for me. Sit in an outdoor shelter. I chose the steps of a pre–Revolutionary War building near Benjamin Franklin's house. Bring a recording of a thunderstorm. If you have an MP3 player, have it playing in ONLY one ear. If you have an old-fashioned tape recorder like mine, place it so one ear will absorb the bulk of the crackling. At times, when reading, it was as if the storm were answering the recorded storm: "Everyone out there listening knows / My body feels so way off the ground / As all the big stores go reaching for me." And set a cup JUST OUTSIDE your shelter, let the cup absorb the storm's water. I brought a metal cup, and set it FAR away from me, hoping to catch more than water. But it only caught water, a delicious cup of storm water. Drink and read, "Of being being sucked absorbed into ever vaster / Networks where history's still being taped and re / -ality tested oh y're just suffering the old imperial / Nostalgia he said but the neo-con retards fucked- / Up my spin without me and I guess I don't know / How to criticize democ-

197

racy value or to just say no!" And place a slice of bread in the storm to absorb the nitrogen from the lightning, and of course the delicious water, eat, and let them become your body, "Now let's recount ourselves in terms of crisis dynamics / Depict the ends of state where history and the seas / Choose me since I see you there my dreamy fuck."

DAVID BUUCK'S *THE SHUNT* (PALM PRESS)

Take your laundry to the laundromat, even if you're fortunate enough to have these machines at home. This is about reading poems while feeling machines in public. Set washer to the longest possible cycle. Sit on it, or have a chair beside it so you can lean into it, press into it. Stare at the book's cover and stare at it even when you think you're tired of staring at it, since it's possible you're trying to trick yourself into thinking you're tired when you're actually disturbed. Imagine those bloody arms and hands belong to someone you love more than anyone else in this world. What's this person's name? Say their name out loud while looking at the book cover. Be disturbed, you deserve it. We all deserve it. This is a cover to refer to while reading. PRESS a cheek to the washing machine, then pause while reading to open the lid, and place a hand inside the soapy water. Just keep it there for a few minutes while reading. Reading, your hand in filthy water trying to get clean. Midway through the book, pause to go outside and STRETCH your body, give a good stretch and yawn if you can yawn, this would be around page 54 with the lines, "We will be naming / the dead and injured / and reading anti-war / poetry. Email but put / 'Anti-War Poetry / Book' in the subject / line to make sure / you're not deleted." The dryer, sit in front of it if it's got a round glass window, sit as close as you can. While reading have the rolling heated clothes with the water sucking from their fibers be the image that frames the book. At some point OPEN THE DRYER and stick your head inside with your eyes closed and FEEL the intense heat and humidity, then close it and go back to reading. You would be surprised that no one really notices you, in case you worry about such things. Everyone's busy, they don't even care to know that you're in the middle of experimenting with your reading. If you feel comfortable enough, invite someone in the laundromat to listen to you read from the book for them, "I think there / are theres here / in my devices / the rigorous buffoonery / the fleshy statistics / the secret minutes / the cathected works."

Button mushrooms are what I bring to this. Any mushroom you want, but button mushrooms are the only mushrooms I enjoy raw. ENJOYMENT is essential! Please do not wash them—they absorb water. Brush them off with a clean, dry towel, that's all. Go out into the fresh air and sun. Take these fungi that have grown in quiet darkness, bring them OUT into the lighted world with you. Find a place to relax. Lie flat on your back, place a mushroom on the crotch of your pants or dress or whatever. If you're naked, GREAT, but be clean: you have to eat these morsels. Spend a little time, with your eyes closed, meditating on your genitals, on the mushroom on your genitals. Then move that mushroom up to your breast for the heart chakra point. Put a new one on your genitals. Rest and meditate again. Then move the first one to the middle of your forehead, the second one to your heart, and yet a third one on your genitals again. Now start reading, but be aware that you are MOVING through the mushrooms a channel of energy UP from your genitals to your mind. Read, "to act in opposition to one's genitals / turn your cock inside out and get a cunt like a prius / vs. take some cuntflesh and get a cock like the wright flyer I / @ kitty hawk / with adverse yaw / wingwarped / circumnavigated / how to fashion / a canard" After reading a little while, pause and take the mushroom off your forehead. Pull off the stem and eat that. Run your thumbs along the feathery gills on the underside of the cap. Press it inside out a bit. Cuntflesh into Cock, back again, back again, then EAT IT! It's delicious, right? Move the mushrooms UP, from heart to forehead, etc., with a new one on genitals. Read, "going around adding -ess to nouns / 'lion-ess' / 'poet-ess' / that's such a load / so that the daffydill yawns back / the one who taught me grk is dead / you want to put them in your lap" Pause and study the mushroom from your forehead, EAT IT, move them up, and keep reading until the delicious book is finished, the delicious mushrooms are finished, "we've all crossed thresholds we don't brag about / iphigenia oxling / when arbolaf dies / one is hailed to arden / as one goes hitherto / asphyxiating along the gowanus / in spite of that rat light / in the gutted yardland / or where jackadaws coo / in concrete galoshes"

GET IN THE DARK. Bring a flashlight into a closet and take pillows and shirts and socks and panties and whatever the fuck you can find to C L O S E all the cracks of light from getting I N there. And put a fan in there, and bring water, and put the fan on Low. T H I S is now the atmosphere for T H I S. It's a good time to praise with utmost gratitude S I G H T ! Is anyone going to be looking for you? Make sure you plan on telling everyone you're going out, to a movie, somewhere, B U T to really have T H I S as T H I S atmosphere, having it as all your own, don't tell anyone where you are. It's none of their business how you absorb poems. These line breaks are more like line cuts, cutting across the page, a good thing the flashlight can trace. Do you have binoculars—do you? I tried this and it was marvelous: so put the book on the other side of the closet, which I did by suspending it with clothes hangers. Then flash the light on the book while reading the page through the binoculars, it's great. It's kind of hard actually, which is great. Every once in a while S H U T O F F the light and sit there in the pool of pitch-black quiet. Then S U D D E N LY flick the flashlight back on and read quickly for a little while to make the reading in your head T H E S O U N D that comes, the light, the reading. "I'm glad for waste, its / ascension, its emotional arc / into the prose of governance. / Dumb hostilities issue forth / from all the movements of yester- / morrow, am I liberal when it / comes to prostitution? No." How is this for you, you know you like dark poetry reading, "At the used frame shop / the cruel chase a world. Dan / Marino from Nutrisystem / tells good carbs from bad."

ERIC BAUS'S *TUNED DROVES* (OCTOPUS BOOKS)

Be fully dressed for this one. Fill a tub for a nice hot bubble bath. Climb in, shoes and all, shirt, pants, even a coat if you want. It's nice to F E E L the warm water soak into the fabric, and fill the shoes, soak into the socks; then, then it hits the skin, ah, time for poetry. By the way, make yourself pee before doing this or your bladder will pressure you out of the tub, unless of course you just want to pee yourself in the tub, it's your choice, don't let me interfere.

This book is perfect for a submerged body, but don't get suds on it, or water, and don't doze off and drown; I'm sure Eric Baus would feel terrible, and I would have to console him and tell him that it wasn't his fault you're so stupid to fall asleep with such a book in hand. In fact you deserve to drown if you fall asleep while reading it. You're not stupid, you're okay, you're fine, but midway through reading the book STAND UP SUDDENLY, maybe just before "THE CONTINUOUS CORNER" section. Enjoy the water falling out of your clothes, drip drip, it's dripping off you, you have a body made MOSTLY OF water, but when it's outside you it drips off, unless of course you peed yourself in the tub, then it's dripping out of you. Enjoying this marvelous book? "When the work was finished, there were no chapters. / The name of the child was It Is Not Here. / It is unlikely this is precise. / To reproduce his mother's voice, hydrogen was added to the body. / For all this activity, the sound was flat."

ACKNOWLEDGMENTS

I dedicate this book to my friends, and it's important for me to say that without them I could never love poetry and this world as I do!

Special thanks to friends who have helped edit and read these pages over the years: Joshua Beckman, Heidi Broadhead, Julian Brolaski, David Caligiuri, Robert Dewhurst, Thom Donovan, Ryan Eckes, Laura Jaramillo, Erica Kaufman, Dorothea Lasky, Debrah Morkun, Eileen Myles, Frank Sherlock, Michelle Taransky, Magdalena Zurawski, Jason Zuzga, and others.

Special thanks to friends who have provided space and opportunity for me to conduct and develop (Soma)tic Poetry Workshops over the years: Greg Bem, Julia Bloch, Jules Boykoff, Taylor Brady, David Buuck, Ryan Eckes, Jeremy Halinen, Rob Halpern, Miguel de Jurado, Erica Kaufman, Kevin Killian, Gregory Laynor, Sueyen Juliette Lee, Steven Manuel, Pattie McCarthy, John Mulrooney, Meredith Nelson, Paul E. Nelson, Tim Peterson, Kaia Sand, Juliana Spahr, Stacy Szymaszek, Michelle Taransky, Eleanor Wilner, David Wolach, and others.

My gratitude to everyone at WAVE who works so hard, and with such devotion, for the books they publish. I never take for granted that there are billions of people on the planet, meaning I never take for granted that I'm lucky enough to actually have my poems published. Thank you so much!

Enormous gratitude to the editors, publishers, dancers, filmmakers, artists, activists, and others who have published and performed pages of this book. Your belief in what I'm doing makes this a true collaboration, and simply saying THANK YOU feels completely inadequate, but THANK YOU ALL! The list below is where and how this book lived before it was this book.

MAGAZINES

2nd Avenue Poetry, Aufgabe, BPM: BRIGHT PINK MOSQUITO, BOMB!, Cannot Exist Magazine, Coconut, Columbia Poetry Review, Ekleksographia, Fence, Gazette le Duc, Glitter Pony, Hilda, Hotel, Hump Day Hustler, Itch, KNOCKOUT, listenlight, Loaded Bicycle, Mad Hatters' Review, MARK(S), MiPOesias, Modo de Usar & Co., Mrs. Maybe, The Nation, notnostrums, P-QUEUE, Pinstripe Fedora, Puppyflowers, SATELLITE TELEPHONE, Sawbuck, Scythe, Sink Review, Spiral Orb, Spittoon, SUPERMACHINE, The Swan's Rag, Thumbnail, TRY, WILD ORCHIDS

ANTHOLOGIES

COME HEAR: The Anthology (The Leslie-Lohman Gay Art Foundation, 2007), *DIVINING DIVAS* (Lethe Press, 2012), *E-X-C-H-A-N-G-E-V-A-L-U-E-S* (Otoliths, 2007), *IMAGINARY SYLLABI* (Palm Press, 2011), *KINDERGARDE* (2012), *NO GENDER: Reflections on the Life & Work of kari edwards* (Litmus Press, 2009), *THE ODYSSEY* (Pocket Myths, 2007), *POETRY TIME* (Poetry Time Press, 2011), *QUEER VOICE* (Institute of Contemporary Art, 2010), *WAR & PEACE: The Future* (O Books, 2007)

CHAPBOOKS

ANOINT THYSELF (Dusie Kollektiv, 2010)

MUGGED Into Poetry (CANNOT EXIST Press, 2011)

(Soma)tic Midge (Faux Press, 2008)

Touch Yourself for Art (MONDO BUMMER Press, 2010)

MANY THANKS ALSO TO

Academy of American Poets, *Evening Will Come*, HTMLGiant, *Jacket2*, Non-Site Collective, Pew Fellowships in the Arts, and Underground Public Library.

Filmmaker and digital artist Courtney Shumway made several films and pieces of digital art from some of these pages.

An excerpt from "THE RIGHT TO MANIFEST MANIFESTO" was screenprinted onto a 72" X 80" picnic blanket by the Philadelphia Exhibitions Initiative.

"DIGIT COGNIZANCE" and "your BANANA WORD MACHINE" were choreographed into dance performances by Eleanor Goudie-Averill of Stone Depot Dance Lab.

"your Zoe Magnifier" was written for the 2012 Philadelphia Museum of Art solo show of photographs by Zoe Strauss.

"your Zoe Magnifier" was also a broadside (Mooncalf Editions, 2011) for *THE REFUGEE READING ROOM* exhibition at Space 1026, which was curated and designed by the artist Amze Emmons.

A portion of "Feast of the Seven Colors" was printed by the F.U.E.L. Collection as part of the 2007 animal rights exhibition *PUPPIES ARE BIODEGRADABLE.* (While I was happy to have been invited to be part of a project that brought awareness to the horrific plight of animals, I was *COMPLETELY SHOCKED AND DISGUSTED* when chicken and beef were served at the art opening! *WHAT THE FUCK!?* When I expressed my outrage to the gallery curators they FORBADE me to read my poems at the event! Apparently we were supposed to be there for the plight of puppies AND NO OTHER ANIMALS! I'm STILL angry!)

The (Soma)tic Reading Enhancements first appeared in Third Factory's *ATTENTION SPAN 2009*.

MP3 files from readings by CAConrad of some of these pages can be found online at *PennSound*. Thanks to Charles Bernstein, Al Filreis, Michael Hennessey, and the many other hard-working people behind *PennSound*

The sapling the antenna, or directive
for our own current?

Engage sparks, do the bicycle exercises, or, maybe HOLD
position in air? YES! Let him run his mouth, it's
what he likes to do anyway. He can say, sing whatever
he wants, so long as we keep the bottoms of our feet
connected around the sapling. In fact do NOT give ANY
additional directions from THIS, let the magic HAPPEN.
His freedom depends upon this
freedom numbers to express himself,
poem as anything. But let's try for sex around
the tree, THAT he will be most happy for direction!

Find a small tree, then prepare the ground with blankets
for you and a partner on both sides of the tree.
Get undressed, completely undressed, then get on
the blankets, facing each other.

Flats of Feet...

Snowmen for the free
real snow, or? Or w
Water ice? January s
one snowman for To
one for me. I gathered

AIDS SNOW FAMILY
for those of us who
loved someone who
died of AIDS

from under the giant sycamore tree on the c
22nd & Chestnut. They should stay in Ya
Until — Summer Solstice. Time to go
memories traipsing from one haunt to the next. (B
new notebook Just for those notes).
Visit; Tommy's old job, 4th & South; the bench
would meet him for lunch; his apartment;
we danced for hours (party, 10th & Pine); where he
his allergy medicine in Chinatown; the table

...e would always art at Essene; the restroom in West Wing, 2nd floor of Phila. Art museum where we h...

...the cement we wrote our names in near Ritz East; will come...

Shopping Mall Trees at Cherry Hill, NJ.

~~Tree~~ magnifying glass — study
The ant seemed to smile
under the magnifying
glass, very sweet.
Oh how monotonous
his routine seems to
be to me. Am I glad
I'm not the ant? I'm
not even glad I'm human, so what
do I want? Why bother asking?

cherry
Blossom
first bud
first leaf
full leaf

Security guard after the
maintenance man interrogated me. She
was much nicer, said "He thinks you're
smoking crack." I told her (just
as I had told him) that I'm writing
a poem. THEY ALWAYS WANT TO KNOW
HOW LONG IT WILL TAKE ME! But she
said they have a security camera
watching me. GREAT! Now my
irritation at having been made paranoid!
     Tiny red spider, feather (sparrow?)

even though there are only seagulls today, circling the garbage bins. Tiny pebbles and the exquisite texture of the bark, the grooves, and a dark ravine where the portions MEET, lock like alligator hide.

(NOT going to the party!)

Graveyard TRIANGLE w/the dead
Find a graveyard where you can sit and
be completely private. ~~[crossed out]~~
Pick 3 objects 1 of them a grave.
Imagine drawing a line which
connects these objects. Meditate
on the triangle. WHAT's inside it.

What would be the contents if it were
a different season? Clouds passing?
Is someone you love dead? Alive? Imagine
them inside.
      Meditate on the many
ways there are to die ————.

      How are they looking? Trance
into this moment longer. PUT some THING
in there which is absurd! Milk bottles
exploding, for instance.
      Can you reach a hand into it
in your meditation and if so what
do you grab, remove, turn up, out, or

The birds nest in the tree has
a dead bird in it, a gray feathered
bird — what is it? Was it?

Make a list of the kinds of
animals you've seen pass,
which was oddest? Sheba.

tell Kathleen the
address for dinner

let Ash know
we may have to
give over that
folder of poems
sooner than later

call mom

NOTES

NOTES